Praxis 10049

Middle School English Language Arts

Teacher Certification Exam

By: Sharon Wynne, M.S.
Southern Connecticut State University

XAMonline, INC.
Boston

Copyright © 2009 XAMonline, Inc.
All rights reserved. No part of the material protected by this copyright notice may be reproduced or utilized in any form or by any means, electronic or mechanical, including photocopying, recording or by any information storage and retrievable system, without written permission from the copyright holder.

To obtain permission(s) to use the material from this work for any purpose including workshops or seminars, please submit a written request to:

XAMonline, Inc.
21 Orient Ave.
Melrose, MA 02176
Toll Free 1-800-509-4128
Email: info@xamonline.com
Web www.xamonline.com
Fax: 1-781-662-9268

Library of Congress Cataloging-in-Publication Data

Wynne, Sharon A.
   Middle School English Language Arts 10049: Teacher Certification / Sharon A. Wynne. -2nd ed.
   ISBN 978-1-58197-269-6
   1. Middle School English Language Arts 10049.   2. Study Guides.   3. Praxis
   4. Teachers' Certification & Licensure.   5. Careers

Disclaimer:
The opinions expressed in this publication are the sole works of XAMonline and were created independently from the National Education Association, Educational Testing Service, or any State Department of Education, National Evaluation Systems or other testing affiliates.

Between the time of publication and printing, state specific standards as well as testing formats and website information may change that is not included in part or in whole within this product. Sample test questions are developed by XAMonline and reflect similar content as on real tests; however, they are not former tests. XAMonline assembles content that aligns with state standards but makes no claims nor guarantees teacher candidates a passing score. Numerical scores are determined by testing companies such as NES or ETS and then are compared with individual state standards. A passing score varies from state to state.

Printed in the United States of America   œ-1

PPST: Middle School English Language Arts 10049
ISBN: 978-1-58197-269-6

TEACHER CERTIFICATION STUDY GUIDE

TABLE OF CONTENTS

COMPETENCY 1.0 READING AND LITERATURE 1

Skill 1.1	Identifying major works and authors of literature appropriate for adolescents 1
Skill 1.2	Interpreting, paraphrasing, and comparing various types of texts, including fiction, poetry, essays, and other nonfiction 6
Skill 1.3	Identifying and analyzing figurative language and other literary elements 14
Skill 1.4	Identifying patterns, structures, and characteristics of literary forms and genres 24
Skill 1.5	Situating and interpreting texts within their historical and cultural contexts 33
Skill 1.6	Recognizing various strategic approaches to and elements of teaching reading and textual interpretation 45

COMPETENCY 2.0 LANGUAGE AND LINGUISTICS 54

Skill 2.1	Understanding elements of traditional grammar 54
Skill 2.2	Understanding various semantic elements 64
Skill 2.3	Understanding subjects relating to the analysis and history of English 67

COMPETENCY 3.0 COMPOSITION AND RHETORIC 72

Skill 3.1	Understanding strategies for teaching writing and theories of how students learn to write 72
Skill 3.2	Recognizing individual and collaborative approaches to teaching writing 82
Skill 3.3	Knowledge of various tools and response strategies for assessing student writing 84
Skill 3.4	Recognizing, understanding, and evaluating rhetorical features of writing and organizational strategies 85

MID. SCHOOL ENG-LANG ARTS

TEACHER CERTIFICATION STUDY GUIDE

COMPETENCY 4.0 LITERARY ANALYSIS 90

Skill 4.1 Describe and give examples of the use of one or two specified literary element(s) present in the stimulus 90

Skill 4.2 Discuss how the author's use of the literary element(s) contributes to the overall meaning and/or effectiveness of the text 90

COMPETENCY 5.0 RHETORICAL ANALYSIS 92

Skill 5.1 Identify and describe and/or give examples of the use of one or more rhetorical elements in the stimulus 92

Skill 5.2 Discuss the degree to which the use of the rhetorical element(s) is effective in conveying the author's point and contributing to the overall meaning of the text 93

Sample Test 94

Answer Key 111

Rigor Table 112

Answers with Rationales 113

TEACHER CERTIFICATION STUDY GUIDE

Great Study and Testing Tips!

What to study in order to prepare for the subject assessments is the focus of this study guide but equally important is *how* you study.

You can increase your chances of truly mastering the information by taking some simple, but effective steps.

Study Tips:

1. Some foods aid the learning process. Foods such as milk, nuts, seeds, rice, and oats help your study efforts by releasing natural memory enhancers called CCKs (*cholecystokinin*) composed of *tryptophan*, *choline*, and *phenylalanine*. All of these chemicals enhance the neurotransmitters associated with memory. Before studying, try a light, protein-rich meal of eggs, turkey, and fish. All of these foods release the memory enhancing chemicals. The better the connections, the more you comprehend.

Likewise, before you take a test, stick to a light snack of energy boosting and relaxing foods. A glass of milk, a piece of fruit, or some peanuts all release various memory-boosting chemicals and help you to relax and focus on the subject at hand.

2. Learn to take great notes. A by-product of our modern culture is that we have grown accustomed to getting our information in short doses (i.e. TV news sound bites or USA Today style newspaper articles.)

Consequently, we've subconsciously trained ourselves to assimilate information better in neat little packages. If your notes are scrawled all over the paper, it fragments the flow of the information. Strive for clarity. Newspapers use a standard format to achieve clarity. Your notes can be much clearer through use of proper formatting. A very effective format is called the *"Cornell Method."*

> Take a sheet of loose-leaf lined notebook paper and draw a line all the way down the paper about 1-2" from the left-hand edge.

> Draw another line across the width of the paper about 1-2" up from the bottom. Repeat this process on the reverse side of the page.

Look at the highly effective result. You have ample room for notes, a left hand margin for special emphasis items or inserting supplementary data from the textbook, a large area at the bottom for a brief summary, and a little rectangular space for just about anything you want.

MID. SCHOOL ENG-LANG ARTS

3. Get the concept then the details. Too often we focus on the details and don't gather an understanding of the concept. However, if you simply memorize only dates, places, or names, you may well miss the whole point of the subject.

A key way to understand things is to put them in your own words. If you are working from a textbook, automatically summarize each paragraph in your mind. If you are outlining text, don't simply copy the author's words.

Rephrase them in your own words. You remember your own thoughts and words much better than someone else's, and subconsciously tend to associate the important details to the core concepts.

4. Ask Why? Pull apart written material paragraph by paragraph and don't forget the captions under the illustrations.

Example: If the heading is "Stream Erosion", flip it around to read "Why do streams erode?" Then answer the questions.

If you train your mind to think in a series of questions and answers, not only will you learn more, but it also helps to lessen the test anxiety because you are used to answering questions.

5. Read for reinforcement and future needs. Even if you only have 10 minutes, put your notes or a book in your hand. Your mind is similar to a computer; you have to input data in order to have it processed. *By reading, you are creating the neural connections for future retrieval.* The more times you read something, the more you reinforce the learning of ideas.

Even if you don't fully understand something on the first pass, *your mind stores much of the material for later recall.*

6. Relax to learn so go into exile. Our bodies respond to an inner clock called biorhythms. Burning the midnight oil works well for some people, but not everyone.

If possible, set aside a particular place to study that is free of distractions. Shut off the television, cell phone, and pager and exile your friends and family during your study period.

If you really are bothered by silence, try background music. Light classical music at a low volume has been shown to aid in concentration over other types. Music that evokes pleasant emotions without lyrics is highly suggested. Try just about anything by Mozart. It relaxes you.

MID. SCHOOL ENG-LANG ARTS

7. Use arrows not highlighters. At best, it's difficult to read a page full of yellow, pink, blue, and green streaks. Try staring at a neon sign for a while and you'll soon see that the horde of colors obscure the message.

A quick note, a brief dash of color, an underline, and an arrow pointing to a particular passage is much clearer than a horde of highlighted words.

8. Budget your study time. Although you shouldn't ignore any of the material, *allocate your available study time in the same ratio that topics may appear on the test.*

Testing Tips:

1. Get smart, play dumb. Don't read anything into the question. Don't make an assumption that the test writer is looking for something else than what is asked. Stick to the question as written and don't read extra things into it.

2. Read the question and all the choices *twice* before answering the question. You may miss something by not carefully reading, and then re-reading both the question and the answers.

If you really don't have a clue as to the right answer, leave it blank on the first time through. Go on to the other questions, as they may provide a clue as to how to answer the skipped questions.

If later on, you still can't answer the skipped ones . . . **Guess.** The only penalty for guessing is that you *might* get it wrong. Only one thing is certain; if you don't put anything down, you will get it wrong!

3. Turn the question into a statement. Look at the way the questions are worded. The syntax of the question usually provides a clue. Does it seem more familiar as a statement rather than as a question? Does it sound strange?

By turning a question into a statement, you may be able to spot if an answer sounds right, and it may also trigger memories of material you have read.

4. Look for hidden clues. It's actually very difficult to compose multiple-foil (choice) questions without giving away part of the answer in the options presented.

In most multiple-choice questions you can often readily eliminate one or two of the potential answers. This leaves you with only two real possibilities and automatically your odds go to Fifty-Fifty for very little work.

5. Trust your instincts. For every fact that you have read, you subconsciously retain something of that knowledge. On questions that you aren't really certain about, go with your basic instincts. **Your first impression on how to answer a question is usually correct.**

6. Mark your answers directly on the test booklet. Don't bother trying to fill in the optical scan sheet on the first pass through the test.

Just be very careful not to miss-mark your answers when you eventually transcribe them to the scan sheet.

7. Watch the clock! You have a set amount of time to answer the questions. Don't get bogged down trying to answer a single question at the expense of 10 questions you can more readily answer.

COMPETENCY 1.0 READING AND LITERATURE

Skill 1.1 Identifying major works and authors of literature appropriate for adolescents.

Prior to twentieth century research on child development and child/adolescent literature's relationship to that development, books for adolescents were primarily didactic. They were designed to be instructive of history, manners, and morals.

Middle Ages

As early as the eleventh century, Anselm, the Archbishop of Canterbury, wrote an encyclopedia designed to instill in children the beliefs and principles of conduct acceptable to adults in medieval society. Early monastic translations of the *Bible* and other religious writings were written in Latin, for the edification of the upper class. Fifteenth century hornbooks were designed to teach reading and religious lessons. William Caxton printed English versions of *Aesop's Fables*, Malory's *Le Morte d'Arthur* and stories from Greek and Roman mythology. Though printed for adults, tales of adventures of Odysseus and the Arthurian knights were also popular with literate adolescents.

Renaissance

The Renaissance saw the introduction of the inexpensive chapbooks, small in size and 16-64 pages in length. Chapbooks were condensed versions of mythology and fairy tales. Designed for the common people, chapbooks were imperfect grammatically but were immensely popular because of their adventurous contents. Though most of the serious, educated adults frowned on the sometimes-vulgar little books, they received praise from Richard Steele of *Tatler* fame for inspiring his grandson's interest in reading and pursuing his other studies.

Meanwhile, the Puritans' three most popular reads were the *Bible*, John Foxe's *Book of Martyrs*, and John Bunyan's *Pilgrim's Progress*. Though venerating religious martyrs and preaching the moral propriety which was to lead to eternal happiness, the stories of the *Book of Martyrs* were often lurid in their descriptions of the fate of the damned. Not written for children and difficult reading even for adults, *Pilgrim's Progress* was as attractive to adolescents for its adventurous plot as for its moral outcome. In Puritan America, the *New England Primer* set forth the prayers, catechisms, *Bible* verses, and illustrations meant to instruct children in the Puritan ethic. The seventeenth-century French used fables and fairy tales to entertain adults, but children found them enjoyable as well.

Seventeenth century

The late seventeenth century brought the first concern with providing literature that specifically targeted the young. Pierre Perrault's *Fairy Tales*, Jean de la Fontaine's retellings of famous fables, Mme. d'Aulnoy's novels based on old folktales, and Mme. de Beaumont's "Beauty and the Beast" were written to delight as well as instruct young people. In England, publisher John Newbury was the first to publish a line for children. These include a translation of Perrault's *Tales of Mother Goose; A Little Pretty Pocket-Book*, "intended for instruction and amusement" but decidedly moralistic and bland in comparison to the previous century's chapbooks; and *The Renowned History of Little Goody Two Shoes*, allegedly written by Oliver Goldsmith for a juvenile audience.

Eighteenth century

By and large, however, into the eighteenth century adolescents were finding their reading pleasure in adult books: Daniel Defoe's *Robinson Crusoe*, Jonathan Swift's *Gulliver's Travels*, and Johann Wyss's *Swiss Family Robinson*. More books were being written for children, but the moral didacticism, though less religious, was nevertheless ever present. The short stories of Maria Edgeworth, the four-volume *The History of Sandford and Merton* by Thomas Day, and Martha Farquharson's twenty-six volume *Elsie Dinsmore* series dealt with pious protagonists who learned restraint, repentance, and rehabilitation from sin. Two bright spots in this period of didacticism were Jean Jacques Rousseau's *Emile* and *The Tales of Shakespeare*, Charles and Mary Lamb's simplified versions of Shakespeare's plays. Rousseau believed that a child's abilities were enhanced by a free, happy life, and the Lambs subscribed to the notion that children were entitled to more entertaining literature in language comprehensible to them.

Nineteenth century

Child/adolescent literature truly began its modern rise in nineteenth century Europe. Hans Christian Andersen's *Fairy Tales* were fanciful adaptations of the somber revisions of the Grimm brothers in the previous century. Andrew Lang's series of colorful fairy books contain the folklores of many nations and are still part of the collections of many modern libraries. Clement Moore's "A Visit from St. Nicholas" is a cheery, non-threatening child's view of the "night before Christmas." The humor of Lewis Carroll's books about Alice's adventures, Edward Lear's poems with caricatures, Lucretia Nole's stories of the Philadelphia Peterkin family, were full of fancy and not a smidgen of morality. Other popular Victorian novels introduced the modern fantasy and science fiction genres: William Makepeace Thackeray's *The Rose and the Ring*, Charles Dickens' *The Magic Fishbone*, and Jules Verne's *Twenty Thousand Leagues Under the Sea*. Adventure to exotic places became a popular topic: Rudyard Kipling's *Jungle Books*, Verne's *Around the World in Eighty Days*, and Robert Louis Stevenson's *Treasure Island* and *Kidnapped*. In 1884, the first English translation Johanna Spyre's *Heidi* appeared.

North America was also finding its voices for adolescent readers. American Louisa May Alcott's *Little Women* and Canadian L.M. Montgomery's *Anne of Green Gables* ushered in the modern age of realistic fiction. American youth were enjoying the articles of Tom Sawyer and Huckleberry Finn. For the first time children were able to read books about real people just like themselves.

Twentieth century

The literature of the twentieth century is extensive and diverse, and as in previous centuries much influenced by the adults who write, edit, and select books for youth consumption. In the first third of the century, suitable adolescent literature dealt with children from good homes with large families. These books projected an image of a peaceful, rural existence. Though the characters and plots were more realistic, the stories maintained focus on topics that were considered emotionally and intellectually proper. Popular at this time were Laura Ingalls Wilder's Little House on the Prairie Series and Carl Sandburg's biography *Abe Lincoln Grows Up*. English author J.R.R. Tolkein's fantasy *The Hobbit* prefaced modern adolescent readers' fascination with the works of Piers Antony, Madelaine L'Engle, and Anne McCaffery.

These classic and contemporary works combine the characteristics of multiple theories. Functioning at the concrete operations stage (Piaget), being of the "good person," orientation (Kohlberg), still highly dependent on external rewards (Bandura), and exhibiting all five needs previously discussed from Maslow's hierarchy, these eleven to twelve year olds should appreciate the following titles, grouped by reading level. These titles are also cited for interest at that grade level and do not reflect high-interest titles for older readers who do not read at grade level. Some high interest titles will be cited later.

    Reading level 6.0 to 6.9

    Barrett, William. *Lilies of the Field*
    Cormier, Robert. *Other Bells for Us to Ring*
    Dahl, Roald. *Danny, Champion of the World; Charlie and the Chocolate Factory*
    Lindgren, Astrid. *Pippi Longstocking*
    Lindbergh, Anne. *Three Lives to Live*
    Lowry, Lois. *Rabble Starkey*
    Naylor, Phyllis. *The Year of the Gopher, Reluctantly Alice*
    Peck, Robert Newton. *Arly*
    Speare, Elizabeth. *The Witch of Blackbird Pond*
    Sleator, William. *The Boy Who Reversed Himself*

For seventh and eighth grades

Most seventh and eight grade students, according to learning theory, are still functioning cognitively, psychologically, and morally as sixth graders. As these are not inflexible standards, there are some twelve and thirteen year olds who are much more mature socially, intellectually, and physically than the younger children who share the same school. They are becoming concerned with establishing individual and peer group identities that presents conflicts with breaking from authority and the rigidity of rules. Some at this age are still tied firmly to the family and its expectations while others identify more with those their own age or older. Enrichment reading for this group must help them cope with life's rapid changes or provide escape and thus must be either realistic or fantastic depending on the child's needs. Adventures and mysteries (the Hardy Boys and Nancy Drew series) are still popular today. These preteens also become more interested in biographies of contemporary figures rather than legendary figures of the past.

Reading level 7.0 to 7.9
Armstrong, William. *Sounder*
Bagnold, Enid. *National Velvet*
Barrie, James. *Peter Pan*
London, Jack. *White Fang*, *Call of the Wild*
Lowry, Lois. *Taking Care of Terrific*
McCaffrey, Anne. The *Dragonsinger* series
Montgomery, L. M. *Anne of Green Gables* and sequels
Steinbeck, John. *The Pearl*
Tolkien, J. R. R. *The Hobbit*
Zindel, Paul. *The Pigman*

Reading level 8.0 to 8.9
Cormier, Robert. *I Am the Cheese*
McCullers, Carson. *The Member of the Wedding*
North, Sterling. *Rascal*
Twain, Mark. *The Adventures of Tom Sawyer*
Zindel, Paul. *My Darling , My Hamburger*

For ninth grade

Depending upon the school environment, a ninth grader may be top-dog in a junior high school or underdog in a high school. Much of his social development and thus his reading interests become motivated by his peer associations. He is technically an adolescent operating at the early stages of formal operations in cognitive development. His perception of his own identity is becoming well-defined and he is fully aware of the ethics required by society. He is more receptive to the challenges of classic literature but still enjoys popular teen novels.

Reading level 9.0 to 9.9

    Brown, Dee. *Bury My Heart at Wounded Knee*
    Defoe, Daniel. *Robinson Crusoe*
    Dickens, Charles. *David Copperfield*
    Greenberg, Joanne. *I Never Promised You a Rose Garden*
    Kipling, Rudyard. *Captains Courageous*
    Mathabane, Mark. *Kaffir Boy*
    Nordhoff, Charles. *Mutiny on the Bounty*
    Shelley, Mary. *Frankenstein*
    Washington, Booker T. *Up From Slavery*

For tenth - twelfth grades

All high school sophomores, juniors and seniors can handle most other literature except for a few of the very most difficult titles like *Moby Dick* or *Vanity Fair*. However, since many high school students do not progress to the eleventh or twelfth grade reading level, they will still have their favorites among authors whose writings they can understand. Many will struggle with assigned novels but still read high interest books for pleasure. A few high interest titles are listed below without reading level designations, though most are 6.0 to 7.9.

    Bauer, Joan. *Squashed*
    Borland, Hal. *When the Legends Die*
    Danzinger, Paula. *Remember Me to Herald Square*
    Duncan, Lois. *Stranger with my Face*
    Hamilton, Virginia. *The Planet of Junior Brown*
    Hinton, S. E. *The Outsiders*
    Paterson, Katherine. *The Great Gilly Hopkins*

Teachers of students at all levels must be familiar with the materials offered by the libraries in their own schools. Only then can she guide her students into appropriate selections for their social age and reading level development.

Adolescent literature, because of the age range of readers, is extremely diverse. Fiction for the middle group, usually ages ten/eleven to fourteen/fifteen, deals with issues of coping with internal and external changes in their lives. Because children's writers in the twentieth century have produced increasingly realistic fiction, adolescents can now find problems dealt with honestly in novels.

Teachers of middle/junior high school students see the greatest change in interests and reading abilities. Fifth and sixth graders, included in elementary grades in many schools, are viewed as older children while seventh and eighth graders are preadolescent. Ninth graders, included sometimes as top dogs in junior high school and sometimes as underlings in high school, definitely view themselves as teenagers. Their literature choices will often be governed more by interest than by ability; thus, the wealth of high-interest, low readability books that have flooded the market in recent years. Tenth through twelfth graders will still select high-interest books for pleasure reading but are also easily encouraged to stretch their literature muscles by reading more classics.

Because of the rapid social changes, topics that once did not interest young people until they reached their teens - suicide, gangs, homosexuality - are now subjects of books for even younger readers. The plethora of high-interest books reveals how desperately schools have failed to produce on-level readers and how the market has adapted to that need. However, these high-interest books are now readable for younger children whose reading levels are at or above normal. No matter how tastefully written, some contents are inappropriate for younger readers. The problem becomes not so much steering them toward books that they have the reading ability to handle but encouraging them toward books whose content is appropriate to their levels of cognitive and social development. A fifth-grader may be able to read V.C. Andrews book *Flowers in the Attic* but not possess the social/moral development to handle the deviant behavior of the characters. At the same time, because of the complex changes affecting adolescents, the teacher must be well versed in learning theory and child development as well as competent to teach the subject matter of language and literature.

Skill 1.2 Interpreting, paraphrasing, and comparing various types of texts, including fiction, poetry, essays, and other nonfiction.

Paraphrasing is the art of rewording text. The goal is to maintain the original purpose of the statement while translating it into your own words. Your newly generated sentence can be longer or shorter than the original. Concentrate on the meaning, not on the words. Do not change concept words, special terms, or proper names. There are numerous ways to effectively paraphrase:

- Change the key words' form or part of speech. Example: "American news **coverage** is frequently **biased** in favor of Western views," becomes "When American journalists **cover** events, they often display a Western **bias**."
- Use synonyms of "relationship words." Look for relationship word, such as **contrast, cause,** or **effect,** and replace it with a word that conveys a similar meaning, thus creating a different structure for your sentence. Example: "**Unlike** many cats, Purrdy can sit on command," becomes "Most cats are not able to be trained, **but** Purrdy can sit on command."

- Use synonyms of phrases and words. Example: "The Beatnik writers were relatively unknown at **the start of the decade**," becomes "**Around the early 1950s**, the Beatnik writers were still relatively unknown."
- Change passive voice to active voice or move phrases and modifiers. Example: "Not to be outdone by the third graders, the fourth grade class added a musical medley to their Christmas performance," becomes "The fourth grade class added a musical medley to their Christmas performance to avoid being showed up by the third graders."
- Use reversals or negatives that do not change the meaning of the sentence. Example: "That burger chain is only found in California," becomes "That burger chain is not found on the east coast."

Literary Techniques to Evaluate

- **Ambiguity:** Ambiguity is any writing whose meaning cannot be determined by its context. Ambiguity may be introduced accidentally, confusing the readers and disrupting the flow of reading. If a sentence or paragraph jars upon reading, there is lurking ambiguity. It is particularly difficult to spot your own ambiguities, since authors tend to see what they mean rather than what they say.
- **Connotation:** Connotation refers to the ripple effect surrounding the implications and associations of a given word, distinct from the denotative, or literal meaning. For example, "Good night, sweet prince, and flights of angels sing thee to thy rest," refers to a burial. Connotation is used when a subtle tone is preferred. It may stir up a more effective emotional response than if the author had used blunt, insensitive diction.
- **Symbolism:** Also referred to as a sign, a symbol designates something which stands for something else. In most cases, it is standing for something that has a deeper meaning than its literal denotation. Symbols can have personal, cultural, or universal associations. An understanding of symbols can be used to unearth a meaning the author might have intended but not expressed, or even something the author never intended at all.
- **Rhythm:** Writing can be compared to dancing, in that it is a balance between words and flow. Rhythm refers to the harmony between the words chosen and the smoothness, rapidity, or disjointedness of the way those words are written. Sentences that are too long may disrupt the rhythm of a piece. Reading text out loud is an easy way to impart understanding of literary rhythm.
- **Rhyme:** Writing with rhyme can be especially effective on reader response. Think about the success Dr. Suess had with his rhyming style. Rhyme is tricky though; used ineffectively or unnecessarily, it can break up the entire rhythm of the piece or fog the reader's understanding of it. Rhyme should be used when it is purely beneficial to the format of the piece. Make sure it is not forcing you to use more words than needed, and that each verse is moving the story forward.

- **Diction:** Diction is simply the right word in the right spot for the right purpose. The hallmark of a great writer is precise, unusual, and memorable diction.
- **Imagery:** Imagery involves engaging one or more of your five senses in your writing. An author might use imagery to give the reader a greater, more real picture of the scene they are trying to depict. Imagery may conjure up a past experience that the reader had (the smell of the ocean, the feeling of their childhood blanket) thereby enriching their mental picture of the scene.

Reading literature involves a reciprocal interaction between the reader and the text.

Types of Responses

Emotional

The reader can identify with the characters and situations so as to project himself into the story. The reader feels a sense of satisfaction by associating aspects of his own life with the people, places, and events in the literature. Emotional responses are observed in a reader's verbal and non-verbal reactions - laughter, comments on its effects, and retelling or dramatizing the action.

Interpretive

Interpretive responses result in inferences about character development, setting, or plot; analysis of style elements - metaphor, simile, allusion, rhythm, tone; outcomes derivable from information provided in the narrative; and assessment of the author's intent. Interpretive responses are made verbally or in writing.

Critical

Critical responses involve making value judgments about the quality of a piece of literature. Reactions to the effectiveness of the writer's style and language use are observed through discussion and written reactions.

Evaluative

Some reading response theory researchers also add a response that considers the readers considerations of such factors as how well the piece of literature represents its genre, how well it reflects the social/ethical mores of society, and how well the author has approached the subject for freshness and slant.

Middle school readers will exhibit both emotional and interpretive responses. Naturally, making interpretive responses depends on the degree of knowledge the student has of literary elements. A child's being able to say why a particular book was boring or why a particular poem made him sad evidences critical reactions on a fundamental level. Adolescents in ninth and tenth grades should begin to make critical responses by addressing the specific language and genre characteristics of literature. Evaluative responses are harder to detect and are rarely made by any but a few advanced high school students. However, if the teacher knows what to listen for, she can recognize evaluative responses and incorporate them into discussions.

For example, if a student says, "I don't understand why that character is doing that," he is making an interpretive response to character motivation. However, if he goes on to say, "What good is that action?" he is giving an evaluative response that should be explored in terms of "What good should it do and why isn't that positive action happening?"

At the emotional level, the student says, "I almost broke into a sweat when he was describing the heat in the burning house." An interpretive response says, "The author used descriptive adjectives to bring his setting to life." Critically, the student adds, "The author's use of descriptive language contributes to the success of the narrative and maintains reader interest through the whole story." If he goes on to wonder why the author allowed the grandmother in the story to die in the fire, he is making an evaluative response.

Levels of response

The levels of reader response will depend largely on the reader's level of social, psychological, and intellectual development. Most middle school students have progressed beyond merely involving themselves in the story enough to be able to retell the events in some logical sequence or describe the feeling that the story evoked. They are aware to some degree that the feeling evoked was the result of a careful manipulation of good elements of fiction writing. They may not explain that awareness as successfully as a high school student, but they are beginning to grasp the concepts and not just the personal reactions. They are beginning to differentiate between responding to the story itself and responding to a literary creation.

Fostering self-esteem and empathy for others and the world in which one lives

All-important is the use of literature as bibliotherapy that allows the reader to identify with others and become aware of alternatives, yet not feeling directly betrayed or threatened. For the high school student the ability to empathize is an evaluative response, a much desired outcome of literature studies. Use of these books either individually or as a thematic unit of study allows for discussion or writing. The titles are grouped by theme, not by reading level.

ABUSE:

Blair, Maury and Brendel, Doug. *Maury, Wednesday's Child*

Dizenzo, Patricia. *Why Me?*

Parrot, Andrea. *Coping with Date Rape and Acquaintance Rape*

NATURAL WORLD CONCERNS:

Caduto, M. and Bruchac, J. *Keeper's of Earth*

Gay, Kathlyn. *Greenhouse Effect*

Johnson, Daenis. *Fiskadaro*

Madison, Arnold. *It Can't Happen to Me*

EATING DISORDERS:

Arnold, Caroline. *Too Fat, Too Thin, Do I Have a Choice?*

DeClements, Barthe. *Nothing's Fair in Fifth Grade*

Snyder, Anne. *Goodbye, Paper Doll*

FAMILY

Chopin, Kate. *The Runner*

Cormier, Robert. *Tunes for Bears to Dance to*

Danzinger, Paula. *The Divorce Express*

Neufield, John. *Sunday Father*

Okimoto, Jean Davies. *Molly by any Other Name*

Peck, Richard. *Don't Look and It Won't Hurt*

Zindel, Paul. *I Never Loved Your Mind*

STEREOTYPING:

Baklanov, Grigory. (Trans. by Antonina W. Bouis) *Forever Nineteen*

Kerr, M.E. *Gentle Hands*

Greene, Betty. *Summer of My German Soldier*

Reiss, Johanna. *The Upstairs Room*

Taylor, Mildred D. *Roll of Thunder, Hear Me Cry*

Wakatsuki-Houston, Jeanne and Houston, James D. *Farewell to Manzanar*

SUICIDE AND DEATH:

Blume, Judy. *Tiger Eyes*

Bunting, Eve. *If I Asked You, Would You Stay?*

Gunther, John. *Death Be Not Proud*

Mazer, Harry. *When the Phone Rings*

Peck, Richard. *Remembering the Good Times*

Richter, Elizabeth. *Losing Someone You Love*

Strasser, Todd. *Friends Till the End*

Cautions

There is always a caution when reading materials of a sensitive or controversial nature. The teacher must be cognizant of the happenings in the school and outside community to spare students undue suffering. A child who has known a recent death in his family or circle of friends may need to distance himself from classroom discussion. Whenever open discussion of a topic brings pain or embarrassment, the child should not be further subjected. Older children and young adults will be able to discuss issues with greater objectivity and without making blurted, insensitive comments. The teacher must be able to gauge the level of emotional development of her students when selecting subject matter and the strategies for studying it. The student or his parents may consider some material objectionable. Should a student choose not to read an assigned material, it is the teacher's responsibility to allow the student to select an alternate title. It is always advisable to notify parents if a particularly sensitive piece is to be studied.

Drawing Conclusions from a Text

A common fallacy in reasoning is the *post hoc ergo propter hoc* ("after this, therefore because of this") or the false-cause fallacy. These occur in cause/effect reasoning, which may either go from cause to effect or effect to cause. They happen when an inadequate cause is offered for a particular effect; when the possibility of more than one cause is ignored; and when a connection between a particular cause and a particular effect is not made.

An example of a *post hoc*: Our sales shot up thirty-five percent after we ran that television campaign; therefore the campaign caused the increase in sales. It might have been a cause, of course, but more evidence is needed to prove it.

An example of an inadequate cause for a particular effect: An Iraqi truck driver reported that Saddam Hussein had nuclear weapons; therefore, Saddam Hussein is a threat to world security. More causes are needed to prove the conclusion.

An example of ignoring the possibility of more than one possible cause: John Brown was caught out in a thunderstorm and his clothes were wet before he was rescued; therefore, he developed influenza the next day because he got wet. Being chilled may have played a role in the illness, but Brown would have had to contract the influenza virus before he would come down with it whether or not he had gotten wet.

An example of failing to make a connection between a particular cause and an effect assigned to it. Anna fell into a putrid pond on Saturday; on Monday she came down with polio; therefore, the polio was caused by the pond. This, of course, is not acceptable unless the polio virus is found in a sample of water from the pond. A connection must be proven.

Comparing Texts

Fiction is the opposite of fact, and, simple as that may seem, it's the major distinction between fictional works and nonfictional works. The earliest nonfiction came in the form of cave-paintings, the record of what prehistoric man caught on hunting trips. On the other hand, we don't know that some of it might be fiction—that is, what they would like to catch on future hunting trips. Cuneiform inscriptions, which hold the earliest writings, are probably nonfiction, about conveying goods such as oxen and barley and dealing with the buying and selling of these items. It's easy to assume that nonfiction, then, is pretty boring, since it simply serves the purpose of recording everyday facts. Fiction, on the other hand, is the result of imagination and is recorded for the purpose of entertainment. If a work of nonfiction endures beyond its original time, it tends to be viewed as either exceptionally well made or perfectly embodying the ideas, manners, and attitudes of the time when it was produced.

Some (not all) types of nonfiction:
- Almanac
- Autobiography
- Biography
- Blueprint
- Book report
- Diary
- Dictionary

- Documentary film
- Encyclopedia
- Essay
- History
- Journal
- Letter
- Philosophy
- Science book
- Textbook
- User manual

These can also be called genres of nonfiction—divisions of a particular art according to criteria particular to that form. How these divisions are formed is vague. There are actually no fixed boundaries for either fiction or nonfiction. They are formed by sets of conventions and many works cross into multiple genres by way of borrowing and recombining these conventions.

Some genres of fiction (not all):

- Action-adventure
- Crime
- Detective
- Erotica
- Fantasy
- Horror
- Mystery
- Romance
- Science fiction
- Thriller
- Western

A *bildungsroman* (from the German) means "novel of education" or "novel of formation" and is a novel that traces the spiritual, moral, psychological, or social development and growth of the main character from childhood to maturity. Dickens' *David Copperfield* (1850) represents this genre as does Thomas Wolfe's *Look Homeward Angel* (1929).

A work of fiction typically has a central character, called the protagonist, and a character that stands in opposition, called the antagonist. The antagonist might be something other than a person. In Stephen Crane's short story, *The Open Boat*, for example, the antagonist is a hostile environment, a stormy sea. Conflicts between protagonist and antagonist are typical of a work of fiction, and climax is the point at which those conflicts are resolved. The plot has to do with the form or shape that the conflicts take as they move toward resolution. A fiction writer artistically uses devices labeled characterization to reveal character.

Characterization can depend on dialogue, description, or the attitude or attitudes of one or more characters toward another.

Enjoying fiction depends upon the ability of the reader to suspend belief, to some extent. The reader makes a deal with the writer that for the time it takes to read the story, his/her own belief will be put aside, replaced by the convictions and reality that the writer has written into the story. This is not true in nonfiction. The writer of nonfiction declares in the choice of that genre that the work is reliably based upon reality. The *MLA Style Manual*, for instance, can be relied upon because it is not the result of someone's imagination.

Skill 1.3   Identifying and analyzing figurative language and other literary elements.

It's no accident that **plot** is sometimes called action. If the plot does not *move*, the story quickly dies. Therefore, the successful writer of stories uses a wide variety of active verbs in creative and unusual ways. If a reader is kept on his/her toes by the movement of the story, the experience of reading it will be pleasurable. That reader will probably want to read more of this author's work. Careful, unique, and unusual choices of active verbs will bring about that effect. William Faulkner is a good example of a successful writer whose stories are lively and memorable because of his use of unusual active verbs. In analyzing the development of plot, it's wise to look at the verbs. However, the development of believable conflicts is also vital. If there is no conflict, there is no story. What devices does a writer use to develop the conflicts, and are they real and believable?

Character is portrayed in many ways: description of physical characteristics, dialogue, interior monologue, the thoughts of the character, the attitudes of other characters toward this one, etc. Descriptive language depends on the ability to recreate a sensory experience for the reader. If the description of the character's appearance is a visual one, then the reader must be able to *see* the character. What's the shape of the nose? What color are the eyes? How tall or how short is this character? Thin or chubby? How does the character move? How does the character walk? Terms must be chosen that will create a picture for the reader. It's not enough to say the eyes are blue, for example. What blue? Often the color of eyes is compared to something else to enhance the readers' ability to visualize the character. A good test of characterization is the level of emotional involvement of the reader in the character. If the reader is to become involved, the description must provide an actual experience—seeing, smelling, hearing, tasting, or feeling.

Dialogue will reflect characteristics. Is it clipped? Is it highly dialectal? Does a character use a lot of colloquialisms? The ability to portray the speech of a character can make or break a story.

The kind of person the character is in the mind of the reader is dependent on impressions created by description and dialogue. How do other characters feel about this one as revealed by their treatment of him/her, their discussions of him/her with each other, or their overt descriptions of the character? For example, "John, of course, can't be trusted with another person's possessions." In analyzing a story, it's useful to discuss the devices used to produce character.

Setting may be visual, temporal, psychological, or social. Descriptive words are often used here also. In Edgar Allan Poe's description of the house in "The Fall of the House of Usher" as the protagonist/narrator approaches it, the air of dread and gloom that pervades the story is caught in the setting and sets the stage for the story. A setting may also be symbolic, as it is in Poe's story, where the house is a symbol of the family that lives in it. As the house disintegrates, so does the family.

The language used in all of these aspects of a story—plot, character, and setting—work together to create the **mood** of a story. Poe's first sentence establishes the mood of the story: "During the whole of a dull, dark, and soundless day in the autumn of the year, when the clouds hung oppressively low in the heavens, I had been passing alone, on horseback, through a singularly dreary tract of country; and at length found myself, as the shades of the evening drew on, within view of the melancholy House of Usher."

Essential terminology and literary devices germane to literary analysis include alliteration, allusion, antithesis, aphorism, apostrophe, assonance, blank verse, caesura, conceit, connotation, consonance, couplet, denotation, diction, epiphany, exposition, figurative language, free verse, hyperbole, iambic pentameter, inversion, irony, kenning, metaphor, metaphysical poetry, metonymy, motif, onomatopoeia, octava rima, oxymoron, paradox, parallelism personification, quatrain, scansion, simile, soliloquy, Spenserian stanza, synecdoche, terza rima, tone, and wit.

The more basic terms and devices, such as alliteration, allusion, analogy, aside, assonance, atmosphere, climax, consonance, denouement, elegy, foil, foreshadowing, metaphor, simile, setting, symbol, and theme are defined and exemplified in the English 5-9 Study Guide.

Antithesis: Balanced writing about conflicting ideas, usually expressed in sentence form. Some examples are expanding from the center, shedding old habits, and searching never finding.

keen mind

Aphorism: A focused, succinct expression about life from a sagacious viewpoint. Writings by Ben Franklin, Sir Francis Bacon, and Alexander Pope contain many aphorisms. "Whatever is begun in anger ends in shame" is an aphorism.

MID. SCHOOL ENG-LANG ARTS

Apostrophe: Literary device of addressing an absent or dead person, an abstract idea, or an inanimate object. Sonneteers, such as Sir Thomas Wyatt, John Keats, and William Wordsworth, address the moon, stars, and the dead Milton. For example, in William Shakespeare's *Julius Caesar*, Mark Antony addresses the corpse of Caesar in the speech that begins: "O, pardon me, thou bleeding piece of earth, That I am meek and gentle with these butchers! Thou art the ruins of the noblest man That ever lived in the tide of times. Woe to the hand that shed this costly blood!"

Blank Verse: Poetry written in iambic pentameter but unrhymed. Works by Shakespeare and Milton are epitomes of blank verse. Milton's Paradise Lost states, "Illumine, what is low raise and support, That to the highth of this great argument I may assert Eternal Providence And justify the ways of God to men."

Caesura: A pause, usually signaled by punctuation, in a line of poetry. The earliest usage occurs in *Beowulf*, the first English epic dating from the Anglo-Saxon era. 'To err is human, // to forgive, divine' (Pope).

Conceit: A comparison, usually in verse, between seemingly disparate objects or concepts. John Donne's metaphysical poetry contains many clever conceits. For instance, Donne's "The Flea" (1633) compares a flea bite to the act of love; and in "A Valediction: Forbidding Mourning" (1633) separated lovers are likened to the legs of a compass, the leg drawing the circle eventually returning home to "the fixed foot."

Connotation: The ripple effect surrounding the implications and associations of a given word, distinct from the denotative, or literal meaning. For example, "Good night, sweet prince, and flights of angels sing thee to thy rest," refers to a burial.

Consonance: The repeated usage of similar consonant sounds, most often used in poetry. "Sally sat sifting seashells by the seashore" is a familiar example.

Couplet: Two rhyming lines of poetry. Shakespeare's sonnets end in heroic couplets written in iambic pentameter. Pope is also a master of the couplet. His *Rape of the Lock* is written entirely in heroic couplets.

Denotation: What a word literally means, as opposed to its connotative meaning. For example, "Good night, sweet prince, and flights of angels sing thee to thy *rest*" refers to sleep.

Diction: The right word in the right spot for the right purpose. The hallmark of a great writer is precise, unusual, and memorable diction.

Epiphany: The moment when the proverbial light bulb goes off in one's head and comprehension sets in.

Exposition: Fill-in or background information about characters meant to clarify and add to the narrative; the initial plot element which precedes the buildup of conflict.

Figurative Language: Not meant in a literal sense, but to be interpreted through symbolism. Figurative language is made up of such literary devices as hyperbole, metonymy, synecdoche, and oxymoron. A synecdoche is a figure of speech in which the word for part of something is used to mean the whole; for example, "sail" for "boat," or vice versa.

Free Verse: Poetry that does not have any predictable meter or patterning. Margaret Atwood, e. e. cummings, and Ted Hughes write in this form.

Hyperbole: Exaggeration for a specific effect. For example, "I'm so hungry that I could eat a million of these."

Iambic Pentameter: The two elements in a set five-foot line of poetry. An iamb is two syllables, unaccented and accented, per foot or measure. Pentameter means five feet of these iambs per line or ten syllables.

Inversion: A typical sentence order to create a given effect or interest. Bacon's and Milton's work use inversion successfully. Emily Dickinson was fond of arranging words outside of their familiar order. For example in "Chartless" she writes "Yet know I how the heather looks" and "Yet certain am I of the spot." Instead of saying "Yet I know" and "Yet I am certain" she reverses the usual order and shifts the emphasis to the more important words.

Irony: An unexpected disparity between what is written or stated and what is really meant or implied by the author. Verbal, situational, and dramatic are the three literary ironies. Verbal irony is when an author says one thing and means something else. Dramatic irony is when an audience perceives something that a character in the literature does not know. Irony of situation is a discrepancy between the expected result and actual results. Shakespeare's plays contain numerous and highly effective use of irony. O. Henry's short stories have ironic endings.

Kenning: Another way to describe a person, place, or thing so as to avoid prosaic repetition. The earliest examples can be found in Anglo-Saxon literature such as *Beowulf* and "The Seafarer." Instead of writing King Hrothgar, the anonymous monk wrote, great Ring-Giver, or Father of his people. A lake becomes the swans' way, and the ocean or sea becomes the great whale's way. In ancient Greek literature, this device was called an "epithet."

Metaphysical Poetry: Verse characterization by ingenious wit, unparalleled imagery, and clever conceits. The greatest metaphysical poet is John Donne.

Henry Vaughn and other 17th century British poets contributed to this movement as in *Words*, "I saw eternity the other night, like a great being of pure and endless light."

Metonymy: Use of an object or idea closely identified with another object or idea to represent the second. "Hit the books" means "go study." Washington, D.C. means the U.S. government and the White House means the U.S. President.

Motif: A key, oft-repeated phrase, name, or idea in a literary work. Dorset/Wessex in Hardy's novels and the moors and the harsh weather in the Bronte sisters' novels are effective use of motifs. Shakespeare's *Romeo and Juliet* represents the ill-fated young lovers' motif.

Onomatopoeia: Word used to evoke the sound in its meaning. The early Batman series used *pow, zap, whop, zonk* and *eek* in an onomatopoetic way.

Octava rima: A specific eight-line stanza of poetry whose rhyme scheme is abababcc. Lord Byron's mock epic, *Don Juan*, is written in this poetic way.

Oxymoron: A contradictory form of speech, such as jumbo shrimp, unkindly kind, or singer John Mellencamp's "It hurts so good."

Paradox: Seemingly untrue statement, which when examined more closely proves to be true. John Donne's sonnet "Death Be Not Proud" postulates that death shall die and humans will triumph over death, at first thought not true, but ultimately explained and proven in this sonnet.

Parallelism: A type of close repetition of clauses or phrases that emphasize key topics or ideas in writing. The psalms in the King James Version of the *Bible* contain many examples.

Personification: Giving human characteristics to inanimate objects or concepts. Great writers, with few exceptions, are masters of this literary device.

Quatrain: A poetic stanza composed of four lines. A Shakespearean or Elizabethan sonnet is made up of three quatrains and ends with a heroic couplet.

Scansion: The two-part analysis of a poetic line. Count the number of syllables per line and determine where the accents fall. Divide the line into metric feet. Name the meter by the type and number of feet. Much is written about scanning poetry. Try not to inundate your students with this jargon; rather allow them to feel the power of the poets' words, ideas, and images instead.

Soliloquy: A highlighted speech, in drama, usually delivered by a major character expounding on the author's philosophy or expressing, at times, universal truths. This is done with the character alone on the stage.

Spenserian Stanza: Invented by Sir Edmund Spenser for usage in *The Fairie Queene*, his epic poem honoring Queen Elizabeth I. Each stanza consists of nine lines, eight in iambic parameter. The ninth line, called an alexandrine, has two extra syllables or one additional foot.

Sprung Rhythm: Invented and used extensively by the poet, Gerard Manley Hopkins. It consists of variable meter, which combines stressed and unstressed syllables fashioned by the author. See "Pied Beauty" or "God's Grandeur."

Stream of Consciousness: A style of writing which reflects the mental processes of the characters expressing, at times, jumbled memories, feelings, and dreams. "Big time players" in this type of expression are James Joyce, Virginia Woolf, and William Faulkner.

Terza Rima: A series of poetic stanzas utilizing the recurrent rhyme scheme of aba, bcb, cdc, ded, and so forth. The second-generation Romantic poets - Keats, Byron, Shelley, and, to a lesser degree, Yeats - used this Italian verse form, especially in their odes. Dante used this stanza in *The Divine Comedy*.

Tone: The discernible attitude inherent in an author's work regarding the subject, readership, or characters. Swift's or Pope's tone is satirical. Boswell's tone toward Johnson is admiring.

Wit: Writing of genius, keenness, and sagacity expressed through clever use of language. Alexander Pope and the Augustans wrote about and were themselves said to possess wit.

Poetic Elements

Slant Rhyme: Occurs when the final consonant sounds are the same, but the vowels are different. Occurs frequently in Irish, Welsh, and Icelandic verse. Examples include: green and gone, that and hit, ill and shell.

Alliteration: Alliteration occurs when the initial sounds of a word, beginning either with a consonant or a vowel, are repeated in close succession. Examples include: Athena and Apollo, Nate never knows, People who pen poetry.

Note that the words only have to be close to one another: Alliteration that repeats and attempts to connect a number of words is little more than a tongue-twister.

The function of alliteration, like rhyme, might be to accentuate the beauty of language in a given context, or to unite words or concepts through a kind of repetition. Alliteration, like rhyme, can follow specific patterns. Sometimes the consonants aren't always the initial ones, but they are generally the stressed syllables.

Alliteration is less common than rhyme, but because it is less common, it can call our attention to a word or line in a poem that might not have the same emphasis otherwise.

Assonance: If alliteration occurs at the beginning of a word and rhyme at the end, assonance takes the middle territory. Assonance occurs when the vowel sound within a word matches the same sound in a nearby word, but the surrounding consonant sounds are different. "Tune" and "June" are rhymes; "tune" and "food" are assonant. The function of assonance is frequently the same as end rhyme or alliteration; all serve to give a sense of continuity or fluidity to the verse. Assonance might be especially effective when rhyme is absent: It gives the poet more flexibility, and it is not typically used as part of a predetermined pattern. Like alliteration, it does not so much determine the structure or form of a poem; rather, it is more ornamental.

Imagery can be described as a word or sequence of words that refers to any sensory experience—that is, anything that can be seen, tasted, smelled, heard, or felt on the skin or fingers. While writers of prose may also use these devices, it is most distinctive of poetry. The poet intends to make an experience available to the reader. In order to do that, he/she must appeal to one of the senses. The most-often-used one, of course, is the visual sense. The poet will deliberately paint a scene in such a way that the reader can see it. However, the purpose is not simply to stir the visceral feeling but also to stir the emotions. A good example is "The Piercing Chill" by Taniguchi Buson (1715-1783):

    The piercing chill I feel:
        My dead wife's comb, in our bedroom,
            Under my heel . . .

In only a few short words, the reader can feel many things: the shock that might come from touching the corpse, a literal sense of death, the contrast between her death and the memories he has of her when she was alive. Imagery might be defined as speaking of the abstract in concrete terms, a powerful device in the hands of a skillful poet.

A **symbol** is an object or action that can be observed with the senses in addition to its suggesting many other things. The lion is a symbol of courage; the cross a symbol of Christianity; the color green a symbol of envy. These can almost be defined as metaphors because society pretty much agrees on the one-to-one meaning of them. Symbols used in literature are usually of a different sort. They tend to be private and personal; their significance is only evident in the context of the work where they are used. A good example is the huge pair of spectacles on a sign board in Fitzgerald's *The Great Gatsby*. They are interesting as a part of the landscape, but they also symbolize divine myopia.

A symbol can certainly have more than one meaning, and the meaning may be as personal as the memories and experiences of the particular reader. In analyzing a poem or a story, it's important to identify the symbols and their possible meanings.

Looking for symbols is often challenging, especially for novice poetry readers. However, these suggestions may be useful. First, pick out all the references to concrete objects such as a newspaper, black cats, etc. Note any that the poet emphasizes by describing in detail, by repeating, or by placing at the very beginning or ending of a poem. Ask yourself, what is the poem about? What does it add up to? Paraphrase the poem and determine whether or not the meaning depends upon certain concrete objects. Then ponder what the concrete object symbolizes in this particular poem. Look for a character with the name of a prophet who does little but utter prophecy or a trio of women who resemble the Three Fates. A symbol may be a part of a person's body such as the eye of the murder victim in Poe's story *The Tell-Tale Heart* or a look, a voice, or a mannerism.

Some things a symbol is not: an abstraction such as truth, death, and love; in narrative, a well-developed character who is not at all mysterious; the second term in a metaphor. In Emily Dickenson's *The Lightning is a yellow Fork*, the symbol is the lightning, not the fork.

An **allusion** is very much like a symbol, and the two sometimes tend to run together. An allusion is defined by Merriam Webster's *Encyclopedia of Literature* as "an implied reference to a person, event, thing, or a part of another text." Allusions are based on the assumption that there is a common body of knowledge shared by poet and reader and that a reference to that body of knowledge will be immediately understood. Allusions to the Bible and classical mythology are common in western literature on the assumption that they will be immediately understood. This is not always the case, of course. T. S. Eliot's *The Wasteland* requires research and annotation for understanding. He assumed more background on the part of the average reader than actually exists. However, when Michael Moore on his web page headlines an article on the war in Iraq: "Déjà Fallouja: Ramadi surrounded, thousands of families trapped, no electricity or water, onslaught impending," we understand immediately that he is referring first of all to a repeat of the human disaster in New Orleans although the "onslaught" is not a storm but an invasion by American and Iraqi troops.

The use of allusion is a sort of shortcut for poets. They can use an economy of words and count on meaning to come from the reader's own experience.

Figurative language is also called figures of speech. If all figures of speech that have ever been identified were listed, it would be a very long list. However, for purposes of analyzing poetry, a few are sufficient.

1. Simile: Direct comparison between two things. "My love is like a red-red rose."
2. Metaphor: Indirect comparison between two things. The use of a word or phrase denoting one kind of object or action in place of another to suggest a comparison between them. While poets use them extensively, they are also integral to everyday speech. For example, chairs are said to have "legs" and "arms" although we know that it's humans and other animals that have these appendages.
3. Parallelism: The arrangement of ideas in phrases, sentences, and paragraphs that balance one element with another of equal importance and similar wording. An example from Francis Bacon's *Of Studies:* "Reading maketh a full man, conference a ready man, and writing an exact man."
4. Personification: Human characteristics are attributed to an inanimate object, an abstract quality, or animal. Examples: John Bunyan wrote characters named Death, Knowledge, Giant Despair, Sloth, and Piety in his *Pilgrim's Progress*. The metaphor of an arm of a chair is a form of personification.
5. Euphemism: The substitution of an agreeable or inoffensive term for one that might offend or suggest something unpleasant. Many euphemisms are used to refer to death to avoid using the real word such as "passed away," "crossed over," or nowadays "passed."
6. Hyperbole: Deliberate exaggeration for effect or comic effect. An example from Shakespeare's *The Merchant of Venice*:
    Why, if two gods should play some heavenly match
    And on the wager lay two earthly women,
    And Portia one, there must be something else
    Pawned with the other, for the poor rude world
    Hath not her fellow.
7. Climax: A number of phrases or sentences are arranged in ascending order of rhetorical forcefulness. Example from Melville's *Moby Dick*:
    All that most maddens and torments; all that stirs up the lees of things; all truth with malice in it; all that cracks the sinews and cakes the brain; all the subtle demonisms of life and thought; all evil, to crazy Ahab, were visibly personified and made practically assailable in Moby Dick.
8. Bathos: A ludicrous attempt to portray pathos—that is, to evoke pity, sympathy, or sorrow. It may result from inappropriately dignifying the commonplace, elevated language to describe something trivial, or greatly exaggerated pathos.
9. Oxymoron: A contradiction in terms deliberately employed for effect. It is usually seen in a qualifying adjective whose meaning is contrary to that of the noun it modifies such as wise folly.

10. Irony: Expressing something other than and particularly opposite the literal meaning such as words of praise when blame is intended. In poetry, it is often used as a sophisticated or resigned awareness of contrast between what is and what ought to be and expresses a controlled pathos without sentimentality. It is a form of indirection that avoids overt praise or censure. An early example: the Greek comic character Eiron, a clever underdog who by his wit repeatedly triumphs over the boastful character Alazon.

11. Alliteration: The repetition of consonant sounds in two or more neighboring words or syllables. In its simplest form, it reinforces one or two consonant sounds. Example: Shakespeare's Sonnet #12:

    When I do count the clock that tells the time.

   Some poets have used more complex patterns of alliteration by creating consonants both at the beginning of words and at the beginning of stressed syllables within words. Example: Shelley's "Stanzas   Written in Dejection Near Naples"

    The City's voice itself is soft like Solitude's

12. Onomatopoeia: The naming of a thing or action by a vocal imitation of the sound associated with it such as buzz or hiss or the use of words whose sound suggests the sense. A good example: from "The Brook" by Tennyson:

    I chatter over stony ways,
    In little sharps and trebles,
    I bubble into eddying bays,
    I babble on the pebbles.

13. Malapropism: A verbal blunder in which one word is replaced by another similar in sound but different in meaning. Comes from Sheridan's Mrs. Malaprop in *The Rivals* (1775). Thinking of the geography of contiguous countries, she spoke of the "geometry" of "contagious countries."

Poets use figures of speech to sharpen the effect and meaning of their poems and to help readers see things in ways they have never seen them before. Marianne Moore observed that a fir tree has "an emerald turkey-foot at the top." Her poem makes us aware of something we probably had never noticed before. The sudden recognition of the likeness yields pleasure in the reading. Figurative language allows for the statement of truths that more literal language cannot. Skillfully used, a figure of speech will help the reader see more clearly and to focus upon particulars. Figures of speech add many dimensions of richness to our reading and understanding of a poem; they also allow many opportunities for worthwhile analysis. The approach to take in analyzing a poem on the basis of its figures of speech is to ask the question: What does it do for the poem? Does it underscore meaning? Does it intensify understanding? Does it increase the intensity of our response?

Skill 1.4   Identifying patterns, structures, and characteristics of literary forms and genres.

The major literary genres include allegory, ballad, drama, epic, epistle, essay, fable, novel, poem, romance, and the short story.

Allegory: A story in verse or prose with characters representing virtues and vices. There are two meanings, symbolic and literal. John Bunyan's *The Pilgrim's Progress* is the most renowned of this genre.

Ballad: An *in medias res* story told or sung, usually in verse and accompanied by music. Literary devices found in ballads include the refrain, or repeated section, and incremental repetition, or anaphora, for effect. Earliest forms were anonymous folk ballads. Later forms include Coleridge's Romantic masterpiece, "The Rime of the Ancient Mariner."

Drama: Plays – comedy, modern, or tragedy - typically in five acts. Traditionalists and neoclassicists adhere to Aristotle's unities of time, place and action. Plot development is advanced via dialogue. Literary devices include asides, soliloquies and the chorus representing public opinion. Greatest of all dramatists/playwrights is William Shakespeare. Other dramaturges include Ibsen, Williams, Miller, Shaw, Stoppard, Racine, Moliére, Sophocles, Aeschylus, Euripides, and Aristophanes.

Epic: Long poem usually of book length reflecting values inherent in the generative society. Epic devices include an invocation to a Muse for inspiration, purpose for writing, universal setting, protagonist and antagonist who possess supernatural strength and acumen, and interventions of a God or the gods. Understandably, there are very few epics: Homer's *Iliad* and *Odyssey*, Virgil's *Aeneid*, Milton's *Paradise Lost*, Spenser's *The Fairie Queene*, Barrett Browning's *Aurora Leigh*, and Pope's mock-epic, *The Rape of the Lock*.

Epistle: A letter that is not always originally intended for public distribution, but due to the fame of the sender and/or recipient, becomes public domain. Paul wrote epistles that were later placed in the Bible.

Essay: Typically a limited length prose work focusing on a topic and propounding a definite point of view and authoritative tone. Great essayists include Carlyle, Lamb, DeQuincy, Emerson and Montaigne, who is credited with defining this genre.

Fable: Terse tale offering up a moral or exemplum. Chaucer's "The Nun's Priest's Tale" is a fine example of a *bete fabliau* or beast fable in which animals speak and act characteristically human, illustrating human foibles.

Legend: A traditional narrative or collection of related narratives, popularly regarded as historically factual but actually a mixture of fact and fiction.

Myth: Stories that are more or less universally shared within a culture to explain its history and traditions.

Novel: The longest form of fictional prose containing a variety of characterizations, settings, local color and regionalism. Most have complex plots, expanded description, and attention to detail. Some of the great novelists include Austin, the Brontes, Twain, Tolstoy, Hugo, Hardy, Dickens, Hawthorne, Forster, and Flaubert.

Poem: The only requirement is rhythm. Sub-genres include fixed types of literature such as the sonnet, elegy, ode, pastoral, and villanelle. Unfixed types of literature include blank verse and dramatic monologue.

Romance: A highly imaginative tale set in a fantastical realm dealing with the conflicts between heroes, villains and/or monsters. "The Knight's Tale" from Chaucer's *Canterbury Tales*, *Sir Gawain and the Green Knight* and Keats' "The Eve of St. Agnes" are prime representatives.

Short Story: Typically a terse narrative, with less developmental background about characters may include description, author's point of view, and tone. Poe emphasized that a successful short story should create one focused impact. Considered to be great short story writers are Hemingway, Faulkner, Twain, Joyce, Shirley Jackson, Flannery O'Connor, de Maupasssant, Saki, Edgar Allen Poe, and Pushkin.

Types of Drama

Comedy: The comedic form of dramatic literature is meant to amuse, and often ends happily. It uses techniques such as satire or parody, and can take many forms, from farce to burlesque. Examples include Dante Alighieri's *The Divine Comedy*, Noel Coward's play *Private Lives*, and some of Geoffrey Chaucer's *Canterbury Tales* and William Shakespeare's plays.

Tragedy: Tragedy is comedy's other half. It is defined as a work of drama written in either prose or poetry, telling the story of a brave, noble hero who, because of some tragic character flaw, brings ruin upon himself. It is characterized by serious, poetic language that evokes pity and fear. In modern times, dramatists have tried to update its image by drawing its main characters from the middle class and showing their nobility through their nature instead of their standing. The classic example of tragedy is Sophocles' *Oedipus Rex*, while Henrik Ibsen and Arthur Miller epitomize modern tragedy.

Drama: In its most general sense, a drama is any work that is designed to be performed by actors onstage. It can also refer to the broad literary genre that includes comedy and tragedy. Contemporary usage, however, denotes drama as a work that treats serious subjects and themes but does not aim for the same grandeur as tragedy.

Drama usually deals with characters of a less stately nature than tragedy. A classical example is Sophocles' tragedy *Oedipus Rex*, while Eugene O'Neill's *The Iceman Cometh* represents modern drama.

Dramatic Monologue: A dramatic monologue is a speech given by an actor, usually intended for themselves, but with the intended audience in mind. It reveals key aspects of the character's psyche and sheds insight on the situation at hand. The audience takes the part of the silent listener, passing judgment and giving sympathy at the same time. This form was invented and used predominantly by Victorian poet Robert Browning.

Tempo

Interpretation of dialogue must be connected to motivation and detail. During this time, the director is also concerned with pace and seeks a variation of tempo. If the overall pace is too slow, then the action becomes dull and dragging. If the overall pace is too fast, then the audience will not be able to understand what is going on, for they are being hit with too much information to process.

Dramatic Arc

Good drama is built on conflict of some kind — an opposition of forces or desires that must be resolved by the end of the story. The conflict can be internal, involving emotional and psychological pressures, or it can be external, drawing the characters into tumultuous events. These themes are presented to the audience in a narrative arc that looks roughly like this:

Following the Arc

Although any performance may have a series of rising and falling levels of intensity, in general the opening should set in motion the events which will generate an emotional high toward the middle or end of the story. Then, regardless of whether the ending is happy, sad, bittersweet, or despairing, the resolution eases the audience down from those heights and establishes some sense of closure. Reaching the climax too soon undermines the dramatic impact of the remaining portion of the performance, whereas reaching it too late rushes the ending and creates a jarringly abrupt end to events.

Types of Nonfiction

Biography: A form of nonfictional literature, the subject of which is the life of an individual. The earliest biographical writings were probably funeral speeches and inscriptions, usually praising the life and example of the deceased. Early biographies evolved from this and were almost invariably uncritical, even distorted, and always laudatory. Beginning in the 18th century, this form of literature saw major development; an eminent example is James Boswell's *Life of Johnson*, which is very detailed and even records conversations. Eventually, the antithesis of the grossly exaggerated tomes praising an individual, usually a person of circumstance, developed. This form is denunciatory, debunking, and often inflammatory. A famous modern example is Lytton Strachey's *Eminent Victorians* (1918).

Autobiography: A form of biography, but it is written by the subject himself or herself. Autobiographies can range from the very formal to intimate writings made during one's life that were not intended for publication. These include letters, diaries, journals, memoirs, and reminiscences. Autobiography, generally speaking, began in the 15th century; one of the first examples is one written in England by Margery Kempe. There are four kinds of autobiography: thematic, religious, intellectual, and fictionalized. Some "novels" may be thinly disguised autobiography, such as the novels of Thomas Wolfe.

Informational books and articles: Make up much of the reading of modern Americans. Magazines began to be popular in the 19th century in this country, and while many of the contributors to those publications intended to influence the political/social/religious convictions of their readers, many also simply intended to pass on information. A book or article whose purpose is simply to be informative, that is, not to persuade, is called exposition (adjectival form: expository). An example of an expository book is the *MLA Style Manual*. The writers do not intend to persuade their readers to use the recommended stylistic features in their writing; they are simply making them available in case a reader needs such a guide. Articles in magazines such as *Time* may be persuasive in purpose, such as Joe Klein's regular column, but for the most part they are expository, giving information that television coverage of a news story might not have time to include.

Newspaper accounts of events: Expository in nature, of course, a reporting of a happening. That happening might be a school board meeting, an automobile accident that sent several people to a hospital and accounted for the death of a passenger, or the election of the mayor. They are not intended to be persuasive although the bias of a reporter or of an editor must be factored in. A newspapers' editorial stance is often openly declared, and it may be reflected in such things as news reports. Reporters are expected to be unbiased in their coverage and most of them will defend their disinterest fiercely, but what a writer *sees* in an event is inevitably shaped to some extent by the writer's beliefs and experiences.

Characteristics of Poetry

The greatest difficulty in analyzing narrative poetry is that it partakes of many genres. It can have all the features of poetry: meter, rhyme, verses, stanzas, etc., but it can have all the features of prose, not only fictional prose but also nonfictional. It can have a protagonist, characters, conflicts, action, plot, climax, theme, and tone. It can also be a persuasive discourse and have a thesis (real or derived) and supporting points. The arrangement of an analysis will depend to a great extent upon the peculiarities of the poem itself.

In an epic, the conflicts take place in the social sphere rather than a personal life, and it will have a historical basis or one that is accepted as historical. The conflict will be between opposed nations or races and will involve diverging views of civilization that are the foundation of the challenge. Often it will involve the pitting of a group that conceives of itself as a higher civilization against a lower civilization and, more often than not, divine will determines that the higher one will win, exerting its force over the lower, barbarous, and profane enemy. Examples are the conflict of Greece with Troy, the fates of Rome with the Carthaginian and the Italian, the Crusaders with the Saracen, or even of Milton's Omnipotent versus Satan. In analyzing these works, protagonist and antagonist need to be clearly identified, the conflicts established, the climax and an outcome that sets the world right in the mind of the writer clearly shown .

At the same time, the form of the epic as a poem must be considered. What meter, rhyme scheme, verse form, and stanza form have been chosen to tell this story. Is it consistent? If it varies, where does it vary and what does the varying do for the poem/story? What about figures of speech? Is there alliteration or onomatopoeia? Etc.

The epic is a major literary form historically although it had begun to fall out of favor by the end of the seventeenth century. There have been notable efforts to produce an American epic, but they always seem to slide over into prose. The short story and the novel began to take over the genre. Even so, some would say that *Moby Dick* is an American epic.

Narrative poetry has been very much a part of the output of modern American writers totally apart from attempts to write epics. Many of Emily Dickenson's poems are narrative in form and retain the features that we look for in the finest of American poetry. The first two verses of "A Narrow Fellow in the Grass" illustrate the use of narrative in a poem:

    A narrow fellow in the grass
    Occasionally rides;
    You may have met him—did you not?
    His notice sudden is.

The grass divides as with a comb,
A spotted shaft is seen;
And then it closes at your feet
And opens further on. . . .

This is certainly narrative in nature and has many of the aspects of prose narrative. At the same time, it is a poem with rhyme, meter, verses, stanzas, etc. and can be analyzed as such.

Types of Poetry

The sonnet is a fixed-verse form of Italian origin, which consists of 14 lines that are typically five-foot iambics rhyming according to a prescribed scheme. Popular since its creation in the thirteenth century in Sicily, it spread at first to Tuscany, where it was adopted by Petrarch. The Petrarchan sonnet generally has a two-part theme. The first eight lines, the octave, state a problem, ask a question, or express an emotional tension. The last six lines, the sestet, resolve the problem, answer the question, or relieve the tension. The rhyme scheme of the octave is abbaabba; that of the sestet varies.

Sir Thomas Wyatt and Henry Howard, Earl of Surrey, introduced this form into England in the sixteenth century. It played an important role in the development of Elizabethan lyric poetry, and a distinctive English sonnet developed, which was composed of three quatrains, each with an independent rhyme-scheme, and it ended with a rhymed couplet. A form of the English sonnet created by Edmond Spenser combines the English form and the Italian. The Spenserian sonnet follows the English quatrain and couplet pattern but resembles the Italian in its rhyme scheme, which is linked: abab bcbc cdcd ee. Many poets wrote sonnet sequences, where several sonnets were linked together, usually to tell a story. Considered to be the greatest of all sonnet sequences is one of Shakespeare's, which are addressed to a young man and a "dark lady" wherein the love story is overshadowed by the underlying reflections on time and art, growth and decay, and fame and fortune.

The sonnet continued to develop, more in topics than in form. When John Donne in the seventeenth century used the form for religious themes, some of which are almost sermons, or on personal reflections ("When I consider how my light is spent"), there were no longer any boundaries on the themes it could take.

That it is a flexible form is demonstrated in the wide range of themes and purposes it has been used for—all the way from more frivolous concerns to statements about time and death. Wordsworth, Keats, and Elizabeth Barrett Browning used the Petrarchan form of the sonnet. A well-known example is Wordsworth's "The World Is Too Much With Us." Rainer Maria Rilke's Sonnette an Orpheus (1922) is a well-known twentieth-century sonnet.

Analysis of a sonnet should focus on the form—does it fit a traditional pattern or does it break from tradition? If so, why did the poet choose to make that break?

Does it reflect the purpose of the poem? What is the theme? What is the purpose? Is it narrative? If so, what story does it tell and is there an underlying meaning? Is the sonnet appropriate for the subject matter?

The limerick probably originated in County Limerick, Ireland, in the 18th century. It is a form of short, humorous verse, often nonsensical, and often ribald. Its five lines rhyme aabbaa with three feet in all lines except the third and fourth, which have only two. Rarely presented as serious poetry, this form is popular because almost anyone can write it.

Analysis of a limerick should focus on its form. Does it conform to a traditional pattern or does it break from the tradition? If so, what impact does that have on the meaning? Is the poem serious or frivolous? Is it funny? Does it try to be funny but does not achieve its purpose? Is there a serious meaning underlying the frivolity?

A cinquain is a poem with a five-line stanza. Adelaide Crapsey (1878-1914) called a five-line verse form a cinquain and invented a particular meter for it. Similar to the haiku, there are two syllables in the first and last lines and four, six, and eight in the middle three lines. It has a mostly iambic cadence. Her poem, "November Night," is an example:

> Listen…
> With faint dry sound
> Like steps of passing ghosts,
> the leaves, frost-crisp'd, break from the trees
> And fall.

Haiku is a very popular unrhymed form that is limited to seventeen syllables arranged in three lines thus: five, seven, and five syllables. This verse form originated in Japan in the seventeenth century where it is accepted as serious poetry and is Japan's most popular form. Originally, it was to deal with the season, the time of day, and the landscape although as it has come into more common use, the subjects have become less restricted. The imagist poets and other English writers used the form or imitated it. It's a form much used in classrooms to introduce students to the writing of poetry.

Analysis of a cinquain and a haiku poem should focus on form first. Does the haiku poem conform to the seventeen-syllables requirement and are they arranged in a five, seven, and five pattern? For a cinquain, does it have only five lines? Does the poem distill the words so as much meaning as possible can be conveyed? Does it treat a serious subject? Is the theme discernable? Short forms like these seem simple to dash off; however, they are not effective unless the words are chosen and pared so the meaning intended is conveyed. The impact should be forceful, and that often takes more effort, skill, and creativity than longer forms. This should be taken into account in their analysis.

Fables, Folk Tales, Fairy Tales, and Mythology

Literary allusions are drawn from classic mythology, national folklore, and religious writings that are supposed to have such familiarity to the reader that he can recognize the comparison between the subject of the allusion and the person, place, or event in the current reading. Children and adolescents who have knowledge of proverbs, fables, myths, epics, and the *Bible* can understand these allusions and thereby appreciate their reading to a greater degree than those who cannot recognize them.

Fables and folktales

This literary group of stories and legends was originally orally transmitted to the common populace to provide models of exemplary behavior or deeds worthy of recognition and homage.

In fables, animals talk, feel, and behave like human beings. The fable always has a moral and the animals illustrate specific people or groups without directly identifying them. For example, in Aesop's *Fables,* the lion is the "King" and the wolf is the cruel, often unfeeling, "noble class." In the fable of "The Lion and the Mouse" the moral is that "Little friends may prove to be great friends." In "The Lion's Share" it is "Might makes right." Many British folktales - *How Robin Became an Outlaw* and *St. George - Slaying of the Dragon* - stress the correlation between power and right.

Classical mythology

Much of the mythology that produces allusions in modern English writings is a product of ancient Greece and Rome because these myths have been more liberally translated. Some Norse myths are also well known. Children are fond of myths because those ancient people were seeking explanations for those elements in their lives that predated scientific knowledge just as children seek explanations for the occurrences in their lives. These stories provide insight into the order and ethics of life as ancient heroes overcome the terrors of the unknown and bring meaning to the thunder and lightning, to the changing of the seasons, to the magical creatures of the forests and seas, and to the myriad of natural phenomena that can frighten mankind. There is often a childlike quality in the emotions of supernatural beings with which children can identify. Many good translations of myths exist for readers of varying abilities, but Edith Hamilton's *Mythology* is the most definitive reading for adolescents.

Fairy tales

Fairy tales are lively fictional stories involving children or animals that come in contact with super-beings via magic. They provide happy solutions to human dilemmas. The fairy tales of many nations are peopled by trolls, elves, dwarfs, and pixies, child-sized beings capable of fantastic accomplishments.

Among the most famous are "Beauty and the Beast," "Cinderella," "Hansel and Gretel," "Snow White and the Seven Dwarfs," "Rumplestiltskin," and "Tom Thumb." In each tale, the protagonist survives prejudice, imprisonment, ridicule, and even death to receive justice in a cruel world.

Older readers encounter a kind of fairy tale world in Shakespeare's *The Tempest* and *A Midsummer Night's Dream*, which use pixies and fairies as characters. Adolescent readers today are as fascinated by the creations of fantasy realms in the works of Piers Anthony, Ursula LeGuin, and Anne McCaffrey. An extension of interest in the supernatural is the popularity of science fiction that allows us to use current knowledge to predict the possible course of the future.

Angels (or sometimes fairy godmothers) play a role in some fairy tales, and Milton in Paradise Lost and Paradise Regained also used symbolic angels and devils.

Biblical stories provide many allusions. Parables, moralistic like fables but having human characters, include the stories of the Good Samaritan and the Prodigal Son. References to the treachery of Cain and the betrayal of Christ by Judas Iscariot are oft-cited examples.

American folk tales

American folktales are divided into two categories.

Imaginary tales, also called tall tales (humorous tales based on non-existent, fictional characters developed through blatant exaggeration)

> John Henry is a two-fisted steel driver who beats out a steam drill in competition.
>
> Rip Van Winkle sleeps for twenty years in the Catskill Mountains and upon awakening cannot understand why no one recognizes him.
>
> Paul Bunyan, a giant lumberjack, owns a great blue ox named Babe and has extraordinary physical strength. He is said to have plowed the Mississippi River while the impression of Babe's hoof prints created the Great Lakes.

Real tales, also called legends (based on real persons who accomplished the feats that are attributed to them even if they are slightly exaggerated)

> For more than forty years, Johnny Appleseed (John Chapman) roamed Ohio and Indiana planting apple seeds.
>
> Daniel Boone - scout, adventurer, and pioneer - blazed the Wilderness Trail and made Kentucky safe for settlers.
>
> Paul Revere, an colonial patriot, rode through the New England countryside warning of the approach of British troops.
>
> George Washington cut down a cherry tree, which he could not deny, or did he?

Skill 1.5   Situating and interpreting texts within their historical and cultural contexts.

American Literature

Local Color is defined as the presenting of the peculiarities of a particular locality and its inhabitants. This genre began to be seen primarily after the Civil War although there were certainly precursors such as Washington Irving and his depiction of life in the Catskill Mountains of New York. However, the local colorist movement is generally considered to have begun in 1865, when humor began to permeate the writing of those who were focusing on a particular region of the country. Samuel L. Clemens (Mark Twain) is best-known for his humorous works about the southwest such as *The Notorious Jumping Frog of Calaveras County*. The country had just emerged from its "long night of the soul," a time when death, despair, and disaster had preoccupied the nation for almost five years. It's no wonder that the artists sought to relieve the grief and pain and lift spirits nor is it surprising that their efforts brought such a strong response. Mark Twain is generally considered to be not only one of America's funniest writers but one who also wrote great and enduring fiction.

Other examples of local colorists who used many of the same devices are Harriet Beecher Stowe, Bret Harte, George Washington Cable, Joel Chandler Harris, and Sarah Orne Jewett.

Slavery

The best-known of the early writers who used fiction as a political statement about slavery is Harriet Beecher Stowe, author of *Uncle Tom's Cabin*. This was her first novel, and it was published first as a serial in 1851 then as a book in 1852. It brought an angry reaction from people living in the South.

This antislavery book infuriated Southerners. However, Stowe, herself, had been angered by the 1850 Fugitive Slave Law that made it legal to indict those who assisted runaway slaves. It also took away rights not only of the runaways but also of the free slaves. She intended to generate a protest of the law and slavery. It was the first effort to present the lives of slaves from their standpoint.

The novel is about three slaves, Tom, Eliza, and George who are together in Kentucky. Eliza and George are married to each other but have different masters. They successfully escape with their little boy, but Tom does not. Although he has a wife and children, he is sold, ending up finally with the monstrous Simon Legree, where he dies at last. Stowe cleverly used depictions of motherhood and Christianity to stir her readers. When President Lincoln finally met her, he told her it was her book that started the war.

Many writers used the printed word to protest slavery. Some of them include:
- Frederick Douglas
- William Lloyd Garrison
- Benjamin Lay, a Quaker
- Connecticut theologian Jonathan Edward
- Susan B. Anthony

Immigration

This has been a popular topic for literature from the time of the Louisiana Purchase in 1804. The recent *Undaunted Courage* by Stephen E. Ambrose is ostensibly the autobiography of Meriwether Lewis but is actually a recounting of the Lewis and Clark expedition. Presented as a scientific expedition by President Jefferson, the expedition was actually intended to provide maps and information for the opening up of the west. A well-known novel of the settling of the west by immigrants from other countries is *Giants in the Earth* by Ole Edvart Rolvaag, himself a descendant of immigrants.

Civil Rights

Many abolitionists were also early crusaders for civil rights. However, the 1960s movement focused attention on the plight of the people who had been "freed" by the Civil War in ways that brought about long overdue changes in the opportunities and rights of African Americans. David Halberstam, who had been a reporter in Nashville at the time of the sit-ins by eight young black college students that initiated the revolution, wrote *The Children*, published in 1998 by Random House, for the purpose of reminding Americans of their courage, suffering, and achievements. Congressman John Lewis, Fifth District, Georgia, was one of those eight young men who has gone on to a life of public service. Halberstam records that when older black ministers tried to persuade these young people not to pursue their protest, John Lewis responded: "If not us, then who? If not now, then when?"

Some examples of protest literature:
- James Baldwin, *Blues for Mister Charlie*
- Martin Luther King, *Where Do We Go from Here?*
- Langston Hughes, *Fight for Freedom: The Story of the NAACP*
- Eldridge Cleaver, *Soul on Ice*
- Malcolm X, *The Autobiography of Malcolm X*
- Stokely Carmichael and Charles V. Hamilton, *Black Power*
- Leroi Jones, *Home*

Vietnam

An America that was already divided over the civil rights movement faced even greater divisions over the war in Vietnam. Those who were in favor of the war and who opposed withdrawal saw it as the major front in the war against communism. Those who opposed the war and who favored withdrawal of the troops believed that it would not serve to defeat communism and was a quagmire.

Catch-22 by Joseph Heller was a popular antiwar novel that became a successful movie of the time. *Authors Take Sides on Vietnam*, edited by Cecil Woolf and John Bagguley is a collection of essays by 168 well-known authors throughout the world. *Where is Vietnam?* edited by Walter Lowenfels consists of 92 poems about the war.

Many writers were publishing works for and against the war, but the genre that had the most impact was rock music. Bob Dylan was an example of the musicians of the time. His music represented the hippie aesthetic and brilliant, swirling colors and hallucinogenic imagery and created a style that came to be called psychedelic. Some other bands that originated during this time and became well-known for their psychedelic music, primarily about the Vietnam War in the early years, are the Grateful Dead, Jefferson Airplane, Big Brother, Sly and the Family Stone. In England, the movement attracted the Beatles and the Rolling Stones.

Immigration

John Steinbeck's *Cannery Row* and *Tortilla Flats* glorifies the lives of Mexican migrants in California. Amy Tan's *The Joy Luck Club* deals with the problems faced by Chinese immigrants.

Leon Uris' *Exodus* deals with the social history that led to the founding of the modern state of Israel. It was published in 1958, only a short time after the Holocaust. It also deals with attempts of concentration camp survivors to get to the land that has become the new Israel. In many ways, it is the quintessential work on immigration—causes and effects.

British Literature

The reign of Elizabeth I ushered in a renaissance that led to the end of the medieval age. It was a very fertile literary period. The exploration of the new world expanded the vision of all levels of the social order from royalty to peasant, and the rejection of Catholicism by many in favor of a Christianity of their own opened up whole new vistas to thought and daily life. The manufacture of cloth had increased, driving many people from the countryside into the cities, and the population of London exploded, creating a metropolitan business center. Printing had been brought to England by William Caxton in the 1470s, and literacy increased from 30% in the 15th century to over 60% by 1530. These seem dramatic changes, and they were, but they were occurring gradually.

The Italian renaissance had a great influence on the renaissance in England, and early in the 16th century most written works were in Latin. It was assumed that a learned person must express his thoughts in that language. However, there began to emerge a determination that vernacular English was valuable in writing, and it began to be defended. Elizabeth's tutor, Roger Ascham, for example, wrote in English.

Luther's thesis in 1517, which brought on the Reformation—an attempt to return to pure Christianity—brought on the breakup of western Christendom and eventually the secularization of society and the establishment of the king or queen as the head of this new/old church. This also brought about a new feeling that being religious was also being patriotic; it promoted nationalism.

The ascension of Elizabeth to the throne also followed a very turbulent period regarding succession, and she ruled for 45 peaceful years, which allowed arts and literature to flourish. Although she, herself, was headstrong and difficult, she happened to have very shrewd political instincts and entrusted power to solid, talented men, most particularly Cecil, her Secretary and Walsingham, whom she put in charge of foreign policy. She identified with her country as no previous ruler had and that, in itself, brought on a period of intense nationalism. She was a symbol of Englishness. The defeat of the Spanish armada in 1588 was the direct result of the strong support she had from her own nation.

Drama was the principal form of literature in this age. Religious plays had been a part of the life of England for a long time, particularly the courtly life. But in the Elizabethan age, they became more and more secular and were created primarily for courtly entertainment. By the '60s, Latin drama, particularly the tragedies of Seneca and the comedies of Plautus and Terence began to wield an influence in England. Courtyards of inns became favorite places for the presentation of plays; but in 1576, the Earl of Leicester's Men constructed their own building outside the city and called it The Theatre. Other theatres followed. Each had its own repertory company, and performances were for profit but also for the queen and her court.

It is said that Shakespeare wrote *The Merry Wives of Windsor* at the specific command of the queen, who liked Falstaff and wanted to see him in love. It was also for the courtly audience that poetry was introduced into drama.

Shakespeare and Marlowe dominated the '80s and '90s; and at the turn of the century, only a few years before Elizabeth's death, Ben Jonson began writing his series of satirical comedies.

Court favor was notoriously precarious and depended on the whims of the queen and others. Much of the satire of the period reflects the disappointment of writers like Edmund Spenser and John Lyly and the superficiality and treachery of the court atmosphere. "A thousand hopes, but all nothing," wrote Lyly, "a hundred promises, but yet nothing."

Not all literature was dictated by the court. The middle classes were developing and had their own style. Thomas Heywood and Thomas Deloney catered to bourgeois tastes.

The two universities were also sources for the production of literature. The primary aim of the colleges was to develop ministers since there was a shortage brought on by the break with the Catholic Church. However, most university men couldn't make livings as ministers or academics, so they wrote as a way of earning income. Nashe, Marlowe, Robert Greene, and George Peele all reveal in their writings how difficult this path was. Remuneration came mostly from patrons. Greene had sixteen different patrons from seventeen books whereas Shakespeare had a satisfactory relationship with the Earl of Southampton and didn't need to seek other support. Publishers would also sometimes pay for a manuscript, which they would then own. Unfortunately, if the manuscript did not pass muster with all who could condemn it—the court, the religious leaders, prominent citizens—it was the author who was on the hot seat. Very few became as comfortable as Shakespeare did. His success was not only in writing, however, but also from his business acumen.

Writing was seen more as a craft than as an art in this period. There was not great conflict between art and nature, little distinction between literature, sports of the field, or the arts of the kitchen.

Balance and control were important in the England of this day, and this is reflected in the writing, the poetry in particular. The sestina, a form in which the last words of each line in the first stanza are repeated in a different order in each of the following stanzas, became very popular. Verse forms range from the extremely simple four-line ballad stanza through the rather complicated form of the sonnet to the elaborate and beautiful eighteen-line stanza of Spenser's *Epithalamion.* Sonnets were called "quatorzains." The term "sonnet" was used loosely for any short poem. "Quatorzains" are fourteen-line poems in iambic pentameter with elaborate rhyme schemes.

However, Chaucer's seven-line rhyme royal stanza also survived in the 16th century. Shakespeare used it in *The Rape of Lucrece*, for example. An innovation was Spenser's nine-line stanza, called the Spenserian stanza, as used in *The Faerie Queene*.

As to themes, some of the darkness of the previous period can still be seen in some Elizabethan literature, for example, Shakespeare's Richard II (III.ii152-70). At the same time, a spirit of joy, gaiety, innocence, and lightheartedness can be seen in much of the most popular literature, and pastoral themes became popular. The theme of the burning desire for conquest and achievement was also significant in Elizabethan thought.

Some important writers of the Elizabethan age:
Sir Thomas More (1478-1535)
Sir Thomas Wyatt the Elder (1503-1542)
Sir Philip Sidney (1554-1586)
Edmund Spenser (1552-1599)
Sir Walter Raleigh (1552-1618)
John Lyly (1554-1606)
George Peele (1556-1596)
Christopher Marlowe (1564-1593)
William Shakespeare (1564-1616)

The Industrial Revolution in England began with the development of the steam engine. However, the steam engine was only one component of the major technological, socioeconomic, and cultural innovations of the early 19th century that began in Britain and spread throughout the world. An economy based on manual labor was replaced by one dominated by industry and the manufacture of machinery. The textile industries also underwent very rapid growth and change. Canals were being built, roads were improving, and railways were being constructed.

Steam power (fueled primarily by coal) and powered machinery (primarily in the manufacture of textiles) drove the remarkable amplification of production capacity. All-metal machine tools had entered the picture by 1820 making it possible to produce more machines.

The date of the Industrial Revolution varies according to how it is viewed. Some say that it broke out in the 1780s and wasn't fully perceived until the 1830s or 1840s. Others maintain that the beginning was earlier, about 1760 and began to manifest visible changes by 1830. The effects spread through Western Europe and North America throughout the 19th century, eventually affecting all major countries of the world. The impact on society has been compared to the period when agriculture began to develop and the nomadic lifestyle was abandoned.

The first Industrial Revolution was followed immediately by the Second Industrial Revolution around 1850 when the progress in technology and world economy gained momentum with the introduction of steam-powered ships and railways and eventually the internal combustion engine and electrical power generation.

In terms of what was going on socially, the most noticeable effect was the development of a middle class of industrialists and businessmen and a decline in the landed class of nobility and gentry. While working people had more opportunities for employment in the new mills and factories, working conditions were often less than desirable. Exploiting children for labor wasn't new—it had always existed—but it was more apparent and perhaps more egregious as the need for cheap labor increased. In England, laws regarding employment of children began to be developed in 1833. Another effect of industrialization was the enormous shift from hand-produced goods to machine-produced ones and the loss of jobs among weavers and others, which resulted in violence against the factories and machinery beginning in about 1811.

Eventually, the British government took measures to protect industry. Another effect was the organization of labor. Because laborers were now working together in factories, mines, and mills, they were better able to organize to gain advantages they felt they deserved. Conditions were bad enough in these workplaces that the energy to bring about change was significant and eventually trade unions emerged. Laborers learned quickly to use the weapon of the strike to get what they wanted. The strikes were often violent and while the managers usually gave in to most of the demands made by strikers, the animosity between management and labor was endemic.

The mass migration of rural families into urban areas also resulted in poor living conditions, long work hours, extensive use of children for labor, and a polluted atmosphere.

Another effect of industrialization of society was the separation of husband and wife. One person stayed at home and looked after the home and family and the other went off to work, a very different configuration from an agriculture-based economy where the entire family was usually involved in making a living. Eventually, gender roles began to be defined by the new configuration of labor in this new world order.

The application of industrial processes to printing brought about a great expansion in newspaper and popular book publishing. This, in turn, was followed by rapid increases in literacy and eventually in demands for mass political participation.

Romanticism, the literary, intellectual, and artistic movement that occurred along with the Industrial Movement was actually a response to the increasing mechanization of society, an artistic hostility to what was taking over the world.

Romanticism stressed the importance of nature in art and language in contrast to the monstrous machines and factories. Blake called them the "dark, satanic mills" in his poem, "And Did Those Feet in Ancient Time."

This movement followed on the heels of the Enlightenment period and was, at least in part, a reaction to the aristocratic and political norms of the previous period. Romanticism is sometimes called the Counter-Enlightenment. It stressed strong emotion, made individual imagination the critical authority, and overturned previous social conventions. Nature was important to the Romanticists and it elevated the achievements of misunderstood heroic individuals and artists who participated in altering society.

Some Romantic Writers:
Johann Wolfgang von Goethe
Walter Scott
Ludwig Tieck
E. T. A. Hoffman
William Wordsworth
Samuel Taylor Coleridge
William Blake
Victor Hugo
Alexander Pushkin
Lord Byron
Washington Irving
James Fenimore Cooper
Henry Wadsworth Longfellow
Edgar Allen Poe
Emily Dickinson
John Keats
Percy Bysshe Shelley

World War I, also known as The First World War, the Great War, and The War to End All Wars raged from July 1914 to the final Armistice on November 11, 1918. It was a world conflict between the Allied Powers led by Great Britain, France, Russia, and the United States (after 1917) and The Central Powers, led by the German Empire, the Austro-Hungarian Empire, and the Ottoman Empire. It brought down four great empires: The Austo-Hungarian, German, Ottoman, and Russian. It reconfigured European and Middle Eastern maps.

More than nine million soldiers died on the various battlefields and nearly that many more in the participating countries' home fronts thanks to food shortages and genocide committed under the cover of various civil wars and internal conflicts. However, more people died of the worldwide influenza outbreak at the end of the war and shortly after than died in the hostilities.

The unsanitary conditions engendered by the war, severe overcrowding in barracks, wartime propaganda interfering with public health warnings, and migration of so many soldiers around the world contributed to causing the outbreak to become a pandemic.

The precipitating event of World War I was the June 28, 1914, assassination in Sarajevo of Archduke Franz Ferdinand, heir to the Austrian throne. Gavrilo Princip, a member of a group called Young Bosnia, whose aim included the unification of the South Slavs and independence from Austria, was the assassin. However, the real reasons for the war are still being debated. In the late '20s and early '30s people felt that the war was an accident that precipitated events that simply got out of control. This was used as a major argument for the organization of the League of Nations to prevent such a thing from happening in the future.

At the same time, Germany, France, and Russia were involved in war plans that created an atmosphere where generals and planning staffs were anxious the take the initiatives and make their careers. Once mobilization orders were issued, there was no turning back. Communications problems in 1914 also played a role. Telegraphy and ambassadors were the primary forms of communication, which accounted for disastrous delays from hours to even days.

President Wilson blamed the war on militarism. He felt that aristocrats and military elites had too much control in Germany, Russia, and Austria, and that the war was a consequence of their desire for military power and disdain for democracy. Lenin famously asserted that the worldwide system of imperialism was responsible for the war This argument proved persuasive in the immediate wake of the war and was a precipitating factor in the rise of Marxism and Communism.

A proposal to Mexico to join the war against the Allies was exposed in February, 1917, bringing war closer to America. Further U-boat (German submarines) attacks on American merchant ships led to Wilson's request that Congress declare war on Germany, which it did on April 6, 1917. Following the U.S. declaration of war, countries in the Western Hemisphere, Cuba, Panama, Haiti, Brazil, Guatemala, Nicaragua, Costa Rica, and Honduras declared war on Germany. The Dominican Republic, Peru, Uruguay, and Ecuador contented themselves with the severance of relations. The entry of the United States into the war was the turning point. It's doubtful that the Allies would have won without the infusion of money, supplies, armament, and troops from the Western Hemisphere, primarily from the United States.

The experiences of the war led to a sort of collective national trauma afterwards for all the participating countries. The optimism of the 1900s was entirely gone and those who fought in the war became what is known as "the Lost Generation" because they never fully recovered from their experiences. For the next few years memorials continued to be erected in thousands of European villages and towns.

Certainly a sense of disillusionment and cynicism became pronounced, and nihilism became popular. The world had never before witnessed such devastation, and the depiction in newspapers and on movie screens made the horrors more personal. War has always spawned creative bursts, and this one was no exception. Poetry, stories, and movies proliferated. In fact, it's still a fertile subject for art of all kinds, particularly literature and movies. In 2006, a young director by the name of Paul Gross created, directed, and starred in *Passchendaele* based on the stories told him by his grandfather, who was haunted all his life by his killing of a young German soldier in this War to End All Wars.

Some literature based on World War I:

"The Soldier," poem by Rupert Brooke
Goodbye to All That, autobiography by Robert Graves
"Anthem for Doomed Youth" and "Strange Meeting," poems by Wilfred Owen, published posthumously by Siegfried Sassoon in 1918
"In Flanders Fields," poem by John McCrae
Three Soldiers, novel by John Dos Passos
Journey's End, play by R. C. Sherriff
All Quiet on the Western Front, novel by Erich Maria Remarque
Death of a Hero, novel by Richard Aldington
A Farewell to Arms, novel by Ernest Hemingway
Memoirs of an Infantry Officer, novel by Siegfried Sassoon
Sergeant York, movie directed by Howard Hawks

The dissolution of the British empire, the most extensive empire in world history and for a time the foremost global power, began in 1867 with its transformation into the modern Commonwealth. Dominion status was granted to the self-governing colonies of Canada in 1867, to Australia in 1902, to New Zealand in 1907, to Newfoundland in 1907, and to the newly-created Union of South Africa in 1910. Leaders of the new states joined with British statesmen in periodic Colonial Conferences, the first of which was held in London in 1887.

The foreign relations of the Dominions were conducted through the Foreign Office of the United Kingdom. Although Canada created a Department of External Affairs in 1909, diplomatic relations with other governments continued to be channeled through the Governors-General, Dominion High Commissioners in London, and British legations abroad. Britain's declaration of war in World War I applied to all of the Dominions, for instance. Even so, the Dominions had substantial freedom in their adoption of foreign policy where this did not explicitly conflict with British interests.

The original arrangement of a single imperial military and naval structure became unsustainable as Britain faced new commitments in Europe and the challenge of an emerging German High Seas fleet after 1900, so in 1919 it was decided that the Dominions should have their own navies, reversing a previous agreement that the then Australasian colonies should contribute to the Royal Navy in return for the permanent stationing of a squadron in the region.

The settlement at the end of World War I gave Britain control of Palestine and Iraq after the collapse of the Ottoman Empire in the Middle East. It also ceded control of the former German colonies of Tanganyika, Southwest Africa (now Namibia), and New Guinea. British zones of occupation in Germany after the war were not considered part of the Empire

Although the Allies won the war and Britain's rule expanded into new areas, the heavy costs of the war made it less and less feasible to maintain the vast empire. Economic losses as well as human losses put increasing pressure on the Empire to give up its far-flung imperial posts in Asia and the African colonies. At the same time, nationalist sentiment was growing in both old and new Imperial territories fueled partly by their troops' contributions to the war and the anger of many non-white ex-servicemen at the racial discrimination they had encountered during their service.

Enthusiasm for the Empire coupled with an increase in nationalism in many of the Dominions came together to create resistance to Britain's intention to take military action against Turkey in 1922.

Full Dominion independence was formalized in the 1926 Balfour Declaration and the 1931 State of Westminster. Each Dominion was henceforth to be equal in status to Britain herself, free of British legislative interference, and autonomous in international relations. The Dominions section created with the Colonial Office in 1907 was upgraded in 1925 to a separate Dominions Office and given its own Secretary of State in 1930.

Canada led the way, becoming the first Dominion to conclude an international treaty entirely independently (1923) and obtaining the appointment (1928) of a British High Commissioner in Ottawa, thereby separating the administrative and diplomatic functions of the Governor-General and ending the latter's anomalous role as the representative of the head of state and of the British Government. Canada's first permanent diplomatic mission to a foreign country opened in Washington, D.C. in 1927. Australia followed in 1940.

Egypt, formally independent by 1922 but bound to Britain by treaty until 1936 and under partial occupation until 1956, similarly severed all constitutional links with Britain. Iraq, which became a British Protectorate in 1922, also gained complete independence in 1932.

In 1948, Ireland became a republic, fully independent from the United Kingdom, and withdrew from the Commonwealth. Ireland's constitution claimed the six counties of Northern Ireland as a part of the Republic of Ireland until 1998. The issue over whether Northern Ireland should remain in the United Kingdom or join the Republic of Ireland has divided Northern Ireland's people and led to a long and bloody conflict known as the Troubles. However, the Good Friday Agreement of 1998 brought about a ceasefire between most of the major organizations on both sides, creating hope for a peaceful resolution.

The rise of anti-colonial nationalist movements in the subject territories and the changing economic situation of the world in the first half of the 20th century challenged an imperial power now increasingly preoccupied with issues nearer home. The Empire's end began with the onset of the Second World War when a deal was reached between the British government and the Indian independence movement whereby India would cooperate and remain loyal during the war but after which they would be granted independence. Following India's lead, nearly all of the other colonies would become independent over the next two decades.

In the Caribbean, Africa, Asia, and the Pacific, post-war decolonization was achieved with almost unseemly haste in the face of increasingly powerful nationalist movements, and Britain rarely fought to retain any territory.

Some Representative Literature:
Heart of Darkness, novel by Joseph Conrad
Passage to India novel by E. M. Forster
"Gunga Din," poem by Rudyard Kipling

Ancient Literature

Between 7000 B.C. and 3000 B.C. critical events occurred that not only led to the invention of writing, thus making possible the emergence of literature, but to the development of human civilization, as well. These critical events included the domestication of animals, the development of agriculture, and the establishment of an agricultural surplus.

These three events allowed the small, nomadic groups of hunters and gathers who had up until then existed in pockets all over the world to evolve into larger, stationary communities. The first of these communities to develop was in an area in the Middle East called Mesopotamia, meaning "Land Between two Rivers," with the two rivers being the Tigris and the Euphrates. This ancestor to civilization as we know it was call Sumer, and the people who lived there and who were to create the wheel and the first written language where the Sumerians.

Perhaps the reason the Sumerians were the first to create so much of what is fundamental to civilization goes back to their unsurpassed ability to create an agricultural surplus. With their position between two flowing rivers, the Sumerians developed an extensive irrigation system, which allowed them to create an abundant surplus. This surplus meant greater economic stability, security, and the ability to support a much larger population within the walls of their city.

Hand in hand with a growing population was the need for governance and specialization. Artisans, governors, builders, regulators, and merchants were needed, as well as priests and temples for the flourishing religion. Keeping track of all this activity required the development of some kind of record keeping. At first, pictographs, or images directly representing concrete objects, were etched into soft clay tablets and allowed to dry.

As time went on, the demand on the record keepers grew from recording how many sacks of barley a farmer brought to the temple to describing in great detail and enthusiasm the exploits of the kings. Thus, with the evolution of the city-state and then the nation, pictographs quickly became insufficient to meet the needs of this new societal structure we have called civilization. Eventually the Sumerians developed symbols not only to represent concrete items such as corn and cattle, but such abstract qualities as courage and love.

http://www.crystalinks.com/sumerart.html (for photo)

Skill 1.6   Recognizing various strategic approaches to and elements of teaching reading and textual interpretation.

The question to be asked first when approaching a reading task is what is my objective? What do I want to achieve from this reading? How will I use the information I gain from this reading? Do I only need to grasp the gist of the piece? Do I need to know the line of reasoning—not only the thesis but the sub-points? Will I be reporting important and significant details orally or in a written document?

A written document can be expected to have a thesis—either expressed or derived. To discover the thesis, the reader needs to ask what point the writer intended to make? The writing can also be expected to be organized in some logical way and to have sub-points that support or establish that the thesis is valid. It is also reasonable to expect that there will be details or examples that will support the sub-points. Knowing this, the reader can make a decision about reading techniques required for the purpose that has already been established.

If the reader only needs to know the gist of a written document, speed-reading skimming techniques may be sufficient by using the forefinger, moving the eyes down the page, picking up the important statements in each paragraph and deducing mentally that this piece is about such-and-such.

If the reader needs to get a little better grasp of how the writer achieved his/her purpose in the document, a quick and cursory glance—a skimming—of each paragraph will yield what the sub-points are, the topic sentences of the paragraphs, and how the thesis is developed, yielding a greater understanding of the author's purpose and method of development.

In-depth reading requires the scrutiny of each phrase and sentence with care, looking for the thesis first of all and then the topic sentences in the paragraphs that provide the development of the thesis, also looking for connections such as transitional devices that provide clues to the direction the reasoning is taking.

Sometimes rereading is necessary in order to make use of a piece of writing for an oral or written report upon a document. If this is the purpose of reading it, the first reading should provide a map for the rereading or second reading. The second time through should follow this map, and those points that are going to be used in a report or analysis will be focused upon on more carefully. Some new understandings may occur in this rereading, and it may become apparent that the "map" that was derived from the first reading will need to be adjusted. If this rereading is for the purpose of writing an analysis or using material for a report, either highlighting or note-taking is advisable.

To *interpret* means essentially to read with understanding and appreciation. It is not as daunting as it is made out to be. Simple techniques for interpreting literature are as follows:

- **Context:** This includes the author's feelings, beliefs, past experiences, goals, needs, and physical environment. Incorporate an understanding of how these elements may have affected the writing to enrich an interpretation of it.
- **Symbols:** Also referred to as a sign, a symbol designates something which stands for something else. In most cases, it is standing for something that has a deeper meaning than its literal denotation. Symbols can have personal, cultural, or universal associations. Use an understanding of symbols to unearth a meaning the author might have intended but not expressed, or even something the author never intended at all.
- **Questions:** Asking questions, such as "How would I react in this situation?" may shed further light on how you feel about the work.

Reading emphasis in middle school

Reading for comprehension of factual material - content area textbooks, reference books, and newspapers - is closely related to study strategies in the middle/junior high. Organized study models, such as the SQ3R method, a technique that makes it possible and feasible to learn the content of even large amounts of text (Survey, Question, Read, Recite, and Review Studying), teach students to locate main ideas and supporting details, to recognize sequential order, to distinguish fact from opinion, and to determine cause/ effect relationships.

Strategies

1. Teacher-guided activities that require students to organize and to summarize information based on the author's explicit intent are pertinent strategies in middle grades. Evaluation techniques include oral and written responses to standardized or teacher-made worksheets.

2. Reading of fiction introduces and reinforces skills in inferring meaning from narration and description. Teaching-guided activities in the process of reading for meaning should be followed by cooperative planning of the skills to be studied and of the selection of reading resources. Many printed reading for comprehension instruments as well as individualized computer software programs exist to monitor the progress of acquiring comprehension skills.

3. Older middle school students should be given opportunities for more student-centered activities - individual and collaborative selection of reading choices based on student interest, small group discussions of selected works, and greater written expression. Evaluation techniques include teacher monitoring and observation of discussions and written work samples.

4. Certain students may begin some fundamental critical interpretation - recognizing fallacious reasoning in news media, examining the accuracy of news reports and advertising, explaining their reasons for preferring one author's writing to another's. Development of these skills may require a more learning-centered approach in which the teacher identifies a number of objectives and suggested resources from which the student may choose his course of study. Self-evaluation through a reading diary should be stressed. Teacher and peer evaluation of creative projects resulting from such study is encouraged.

5. Reading aloud before the entire class as a formal means of teacher evaluation should be phased out in favor of one-to-one tutoring or peer-assisted reading. Occasional sharing of favored selections by both teacher and willing students is a good oral interpretation basic.

Reading emphasis in high school

Students in high school literature classes should focus on interpretive and critical reading. Teachers should guide the study of the elements of inferential (interpretive) reading - drawing conclusions, predicting outcomes, and recognizing examples of specific genre characteristics, for example - and critical reading to judge the quality of the writer's work against recognized standards. At this level students should understand the skills of language and reading that they are expected to master and be able to evaluate their own progress.

Strategies

1. The teacher becomes more facilitator than instructor - helping the student to make a diagnosis of his own strengths and weaknesses, keeping a record of progress, and interacting with other students and the teacher in practicing skills.

2. Despite the requisites and prerequisites of most literature courses, students should be encouraged to pursue independent study and enrichment reading.

3. Ample opportunities should be provided for oral interpretation of literature, special projects in creative dramatics, writing for publication in school literary magazines or newspapers, and speech/debate activities. A student portfolio provides for teacher and peer evaluation.

Tracing an idea through a passage goes much better if a strategy if developed for doing so. Good readers usually have these strategies even though they might not be aware of them. A good way to start is by looking for words or phrases that appear more than once or even many times. Following those key words and phrases will make it possible to observe a picture of the idea as it appears in the piece of writing.

Also, most published writers avoid repetition. For that reason, key words in a piece of writing will probably have several synonyms or even more. In strategizing for reading materials for comprehension, this device can be very useful. By focusing on the key words and thinking about their meanings, following the idea will be expedited.

Transitional words and phrases are designed to lead the reader forward and through a piece of writing. Such words as therefore, however, even so, although, etc. are clues to connections between one part of the writing and another and the nature of the connection. Phrases sometimes substitute for words. Some examples, as a matter of fact, in the long run, looking back, etc.

Identification of common morphemes, prefixes, and suffixes

This aspect of vocabulary development is to help students look for structural elements within words which they can use independently to help them determine meaning.

The terms listed below are generally recognized as the key structural analysis components.

Root words: A root word is a word from which another word is developed. The second word can be said to have its "root" in the first. This structural component nicely lends itself to a tree with roots illustration which can concretize the meaning for students. Students may also want to literally construct root words using cardboard trees and/or actual roots from plants to create word family models. This is a lovely way to help students own their root words.

Base words: A stand-alone linguistic unit which can not be deconstructed or broken down into smaller words. For example, in the word "re-tell," the base word is "tell."

Contractions: These are shortened forms of two words in which a letter or letters have been deleted. These deleted letters have been replaced by an apostrophe.

Prefixes: These are beginning units of meaning which can be added (the vocabulary word for this type of structural adding is "affixed") to a base word or root word. They can not stand alone. They are also sometimes known as "bound morphemes," meaning that they can not stand alone as a base word.

Suffixes: These are ending units of meaning which can be "affixed" or added on to the ends of root or base words. Suffixes transform the original meanings of base and root words. Like prefixes, they are also known as "bound morphemes," because they can not stand alone as words.

Compound words: Occur when two or more base words are connected to form a new word. The meaning of the new word is in some way connected with that of the base word.

Inflectional endings: Are types are suffixes that impart a new meaning to the base or root word. These endings in particular change the gender, number, tense, or form of the base or root words. Just like other suffixes, these are also termed "bound morphemes."

Learning approach

Early theories of language development were formulated from learning theory research. The assumption was that language development evolved from learning the rules of language structures and applying them through imitation and reinforcement. This approach also assumed that language, cognitive, and social developments were independent of each other. Thus, children were expected to learn language from patterning after adults who spoke and wrote Standard English. No allowance was made for communication through child jargon, idiomatic expressions, or grammatical and mechanical errors resulting from too strict adherence to the rules of inflection (*childs* instead of *children*) or conjugation (*runned* instead of *ran*). No association was made between physical and operational development and language mastery.

Linguistic approach

Studies spearheaded by Noam Chomsky in the 1950s formulated the theory that language ability is innate and develops through natural human maturation as environmental stimuli trigger acquisition of syntactical structures appropriate to each exposure level. The assumption of a hierarchy of syntax downplayed the significance of semantics. Because of the complexity of syntax and the relative speed with which children acquire language, linguists attributed language development to biological rather than cognitive or social influences.

Cognitive approach

Researchers in the 1970s proposed that language knowledge derives from both syntactic and semantic structures. Drawing on the studies of Piaget and other cognitive learning theorists (see Skill 4.7), supporters of the cognitive approach maintained that children acquire knowledge of linguistic structures after they have acquired the cognitive structures necessary to process language. For example, joining words for specific meaning necessitates sensory motor intelligence. The child must be able to coordinate movement and recognize objects before she can identify words to name the objects or word groups to describe the actions performed with those objects.

Adolescents must have developed the mental abilities for <u>organizing concepts as well as concrete operations</u>, <u>predicting outcomes</u>, and <u>theorizing</u> before they can assimilate and verbalize complex sentence structures, choose vocabulary for particular nuances of meaning, and examine semantic structures for tone and manipulative effect.

Sociocognitive approach

Other theorists in the 1970s proposed that language development results from sociolinguistic competence. Language, cognitive, and social knowledge are interactive elements of total human development. Emphasis on verbal communication as the medium for language expression resulted in the inclusion of speech activities in most language arts curricula.

Unlike previous approaches, the sociocognitive allowed that determining the appropriateness of language in given situations for specific listeners is as important as understanding semantic and syntactic structures. By engaging in conversation, children at all stages of development have opportunities to test their language skills, receive feedback, and make modifications. As a social activity, conversation is as structured by social order as grammar is structured by the rules of syntax. Conversation satisfies the learner's need to be heard and understood and to influence others. Thus, his choices of vocabulary, tone, and content are dictated by his ability to assess the language knowledge of his listeners. He is constantly applying his cognitive skills to using language in a social interaction. If the capacity to acquire language is inborn, without an environment in which to practice language, a child would not pass beyond grunts and gestures as did primitive man.

Of course, the varying degrees of environmental stimuli to which children are exposed at all age levels creates a slower or faster development of language. Some children are prepared to articulate concepts and recognize symbolism by the time they enter fifth grade because they have been exposed to challenging reading and conversations with well-spoken adults at home or in their social groups. Others are still trying to master the sight recognition skills and are not yet ready to combine words in complex patterns.

Concerns for the teacher

Because teachers must, by virtue of tradition and the dictates of the curriculum, teach grammar, usage, and writing as well as reading and later literature, the problem becomes when to teach what to whom. The profusion of approaches to teaching grammar alone are mind-boggling. In the universities, we learn about transformational grammar, stratification grammar, sectoral grammar, etc. But in practice, most teachers, supported by presentations in textbooks and by the methods they learned themselves, keep coming back to the same traditional prescriptive approach - read and imitate - or structural approach - learn the parts of speech, the parts of sentence, punctuation rules, sentence patterns. After enough of the terminology and rules are stored in the brain, then we learn to write and speak. For some educators, the best solution is the worst - don't teach grammar at all.

The same problems occur in teaching usage. How much can we demand students communicate in only Standard English? Different schools of thought suggest that a study of dialect and idiom and recognition of various jargons is a vital part of language development. Social pressures, especially on students in middle and junior high schools, to be accepted within their peer groups and to speak the non-standard language spoken outside the school make adolescents resistant to the corrective, remedial approach. In many communities where the immigrant populations are high, new words are entering English from other languages even as words and expressions that were common when we were children have become rare or obsolete.

Regardless of differences of opinion concerning language development, it is safe to say that a language arts teacher will be most effective using the styles and approaches with which she is most comfortable. And, if she subscribes to a student-centered approach, she may find that the students have a lot to teach her and each other. Moffett and Wagner in the Fourth Edition of *Student-centered Language Arts K-12* stress the three I's: individualization, interaction, and integration. Essentially, they are supporting the socio-cognitive approach to language development. By providing an opportunity for the student to select his own activities and resources, his instruction is individualized. By centering on and teaching each other, students are interactive. Finally, by allowing students to synthesize a variety of knowledge structures, they integrate them. The teacher's role becomes that of a facilitator.

Benefits of the socio-cognitive approach

This approach has tended to guide the whole language movement, currently in fashion. Most basal readers utilize an integrated, cross-curricular approach to successful grammar, language, and usage. Reinforcement becomes an intradepartmental responsibility. Language incorporates diction and terminology across the curriculum. Standard usage is encouraged and supported by both the core classroom textbooks and current software for technology. Teachers need to acquaint themselves with the computer capabilities in their school district and at their individual school sites. Advances in new technologies require the teacher to familiarize herself with programs that would serve her students' needs. Students respond enthusiastically to technology. Several highly effective programs are available in various formats to assist students with initial instruction or remediation. Grammar texts, such as the Warriner's series, employ various methods to reach individual learning styles. The school library media center should become a focal point for individual exploration.

Second Language Learners

Students who are raised in homes where English is not the first language and/or where standard English is not spoken, may have difficulty with hearing the difference between similar sounding words like "send" and "sent."

Any student, who is not in an environment where English phonology operates, may have difficulty perceiving and demonstrating the differences between English language phonemes. If students can not hear the difference between words that "sound the same" like "grow" and "glow," they will be confused when these words appear in a print context. This confusion will of course, sadly, impact their comprehension.

Considerations for teaching to English Language Learners include recognition by the teacher that what works for the English language speaking student from an English language speaking family, does not necessarily work in other languages.

Research recommends that ELL students learn to read initially in their first language. It has been found that a priority for ELL should be learning to speak English before being taught to read English. Research supports oral language development, since it lays the foundation for phonological awareness.

Children who learn to read on schedule and who are avid readers have been seen to have superior vocabularies compared to other children their age. The reason for this is that in order to understand what they read, they often must determine the meaning for a word based on its context. Children who constantly turn to a dictionary for the meaning of a word they don't know will not have this advantage.

This is an important clue for providing students the kinds of exercises and helps they need in order to develop their vocabularies. Learning vocabulary lists is useful, of course, but much less efficient than exercises in determining meaning on the basis of context. It requires an entirely different kind of thinking and learning. Poetry is also useful for developing vocabulary exercises for children, especially rhymed poetry, where the pronunciation of a term may be deduced by what the poet intended for it to rhyme with. In some poets of earlier periods, the teacher may need to intervene because some of the words that would have rhymed when the poem was written do not rhyme in today's English. Even so, this is a good opportunity to help children understand some of the important principles about their constantly-changing language.

Another good exercise for developing vocabulary is the crossword puzzle. A child's ability to think in terms of analogy is a step upward toward mature language understanding and use. The teacher may construct crossword puzzles using items from the class such as students' names or the terms from their literature or language lessons.

TEACHER CERTIFICATION STUDY GUIDE

COMPETENCY 2.0 LANGUAGE AND LINGUISTICS

Skill 2.1 Understanding elements of traditional grammar.

Sentence completeness

Avoid fragments and run-on sentences. Recognition of sentence elements necessary to make a complete thought, proper use of independent and dependent clauses (see *Use correct coordination and subordination*), and proper punctuation will correct such errors.

Sentence structure

Recognize simple, compound, complex, and compound-complex sentences. Use dependent (subordinate) and independent clauses correctly to create these sentence structures.

Simple	Joyce wrote a letter.
Compound	Joyce wrote a letter, and Dot drew a picture.
Complex	While Joyce wrote a letter, Dot drew a picture.
Compound/Complex	When Mother asked the girls to demonstrate their new-found skills, Joyce wrote a letter, and Dot drew a picture.

Note: Do **not** confuse compound sentence elements with compound sentences.

> Simple sentence with compound subject
> Joyce and Dot wrote letters.
> The girl in row three and the boy next to her were passing notes across the aisle.

> Simple sentence with compound predicate
> Joyce wrote letters and drew pictures.
> The captain of the high school debate team graduated with honors and studied broadcast journalism in college.

> Simple sentence with compound object of preposition
> Coleen graded the students' essays for style and mechanical accuracy.

Parallelism

Recognize parallel structures using phrases (prepositional, gerund, participial, and infinitive) and omissions from sentences that create the lack of parallelism.

MID. SCHOOL ENG-LANG ARTS   54

Prepositional phrase/single modifier

Incorrect: Coleen ate the ice cream with enthusiasm and hurriedly.
Correct: Coleen ate the ice cream with enthusiasm and in a hurry.
Correct: Coleen ate the ice cream enthusiastically and hurriedly.

Participial phrase/infinitive phrase

Incorrect: After hiking for hours and to sweat profusely, Joe sat down to rest and drinking water.
Correct: After hiking for hours and sweating profusely, Joe sat down to rest and drink water.

Recognition of dangling modifiers

Dangling phrases are attached to sentence parts in such a way they create ambiguity and incorrectness of meaning.

Participial phrase

Incorrect: Hanging from her skirt, Dot tugged at a loose thread.
Correct: Dot tugged at a loose thread hanging from her skirt.

Incorrect: Relaxing in the bathtub, the telephone rang.
Correct: While I was relaxing in the bathtub, the telephone rang.

Infinitive phrase

Incorrect: To improve his behavior, the dean warned Fred.
Correct: The dean warned Fred to improve his behavior.

Prepositional phrase

Incorrect: On the floor, Father saw the dog eating table scraps.
Correct: Father saw the dog eating table scraps on the floor.

Recognition of syntactical redundancy or omission

These errors occur when superfluous words have been added to a sentence or key words have been omitted from a sentence.

Redundancy
Incorrect: Joyce made sure that when her plane arrived that she retrieved all of her luggage.
Correct: Joyce made sure that when her plane arrived she retrieved all of her luggage.

Incorrect: He was a mere skeleton of his former self.
Correct: He was a skeleton of his former self.

Omission

Incorrect: Dot opened her book, recited her textbook, and answered the teacher's subsequent question.
Correct: Dot opened her book, recited from the textbook, and answered the teacher's subsequent question.

Avoidance of double negatives

This error occurs from positioning two negatives that, in fact, cancel each other in meaning.

Incorrect: Harold couldn't care less whether he passes this class.
Correct: Harold could care less whether he passes this class.

Incorrect: Dot didn't have no double negatives in her paper.
Correct: Dot didn't have any double negatives in her paper.

Types of Clauses

Clauses are connected word groups that are composed of *at least* one subject and one verb. (A subject is the doer of an action or the element that is being joined. A verb conveys either the action or the link.)

Students are waiting for the start of the assembly.
Subject   Verb

At the end of the play, students wait for the curtain to come down.
                  Subject Verb

Clauses can be independent or dependent.

Independent clauses can stand alone or can be joined to other clauses.

Independent clause	for	
	and	
	nor	
Independent clause,	but	Independent clause
	or	
	yet	
	so	

Independent clause   ;   Independent clause

Dependent clause   ,   Independent clause

Independent clause   Dependent clause

Dependent clauses, by definition, contain at least one subject and one verb. However, they cannot stand alone as a complete sentence. They are structurally dependent on the main clause.

There are two types of dependent clauses: (1) those with a subordinating conjunction, and (2) those with a relative pronoun

Sample coordinating conjunctions:
Although
When
If
Unless
Because

Unless a cure is discovered, many more people will die of the disease.
    Dependent clause   +   Independent clause

Sample relative pronouns:
Who
Whom
Which
That

The White House has an official website, which contains press releases, news updates, and biographies of the President and Vice-President.
(Independent clause + relative pronoun + relative dependent clause)

Misplaced and Dangling Modifiers

Particular phrases that are not placed near the one word they modify often result in misplaced modifiers. Particular phrases that do not relate to the subject being modified result in dangling modifiers.

Error: Weighing the options carefully, a decision was made regarding the punishment of the convicted murderer.

Problem: Who is weighing the options? No one capable of weighing is named in the sentence; thus, the participle phrase weighing the options carefully dangles. This problem can be corrected by adding a subject of the sentence capable of doing the action.

Correction: Weighing the options carefully, the judge made a decision regarding the punishment of the convicted murderer.

Error: Returning to my favorite watering hole, brought back many fond memories.

Problem: The person who returned is never indicated, and the participle phrase dangles. This problem can be corrected by creating a dependent clause from the modifying phrase.

Correction: When I returned to my favorite watering hole, many fond memories came back to me.

Error: One damaged house stood only to remind townspeople of the hurricane.

Problem: The placement of the misplaced modifier *only* suggests that the sole reason the house remained was to serve as a reminder. The faulty modifier creates ambiguity.

Correction: Only one damaged house stood, reminding townspeople of the hurricane.

Spelling

Concentration in this section will be on spelling plurals and possessives. The multiplicity and complexity of spelling rules based on phonics, letter doubling, and exceptions to rules - not mastered by adulthood - should be replaced by a good dictionary. As spelling mastery is also difficult for adolescents, our recommendation is the same. Learning the use of a dictionary and thesaurus will be a more rewarding use of time.

Most plurals of nouns that end in hard consonants or hard consonant sounds followed by a silent *e* are made by adding *s*. Some words ending in vowels only add *s*.

fingers, numerals, banks, bugs, riots, homes, gates, radios, bananas

Nouns that end in soft consonant sounds *s, j, x, z, ch,* and *sh,* add *es.* Some nouns ending in *o* add es.

dresses, waxes, churches, brushes, tomatoes, potatoes

Nouns ending in *y* preceded by a vowel just add *s*.

boys, alleys

Nouns ending in *y* preceded by a consonant change the *y* to *i* and add *es*.

    babies, corollaries, frugalities, poppies

Some nouns plurals are formed irregularly or remain the same.

    sheep, deer, children, leaves, oxen

Some nouns derived from foreign words, especially Latin, may make their plurals in two different ways - one of them Anglicized. Sometimes, the meanings are the same; other times, the two plurals are used in slightly different contexts. It is always wise to consult the dictionary.

    appendices, appendixes   criterion, criteria
    indexes, indices   crisis, crises

Make the plurals of closed (solid) compound words in the usual way except for words ending in *ful* which make their plurals on the root word.

    timelines, hairpins, cupsful

Make the plurals of open or hyphenated compounds by adding the change in inflection to the word that changes in number.

    fathers-in-law, courts-martial, masters of art, doctors of medicine

Make the plurals of letters, numbers, and abbreviations by adding *s*.

    fives and tens, IBMs, 1990s, *p*s and *q*s (Note that letters are italicized.)

Capitalization

Capitalize all proper names of persons (including specific organizations or agencies of government); places (countries, states, cities, parks, and specific geographical areas); and things (political parties, structures, historical and cultural terms, and calendar and time designations); and religious terms (any deity, revered person or group, sacred writings).

    Percy Bysshe Shelley, Argentina, Mount Rainier National Park, Grand Canyon, League of Nations, the Sears Tower, Birmingham, Lyric Theater, Americans, Midwesterners, Democrats, Renaissance, Boy Scouts of America, Easter, God, Bible, Dead Sea Scrolls, Koran

Capitalize proper adjectives and titles used with proper names.

California gold rush, President John Adams, French fries, Homeric epic, Romanesque architecture, Senator John Glenn

Note: Some words that represent titles and offices are not capitalized unless used with a proper name.

Capitalized	Not Capitalized
Congressman McKay	the congressman from Florida
Commander Alger	commander of the Pacific Fleet
Queen Elizabeth	the queen of England

Capitalize all main words in titles of works of literature, art, and music. (See "Using Italics" in the Punctuation section.)

The candidate should be cognizant of proper rules and conventions of punctuation, capitalization, and spelling. Competency exams will generally test the ability to apply the more advanced skills; thus, a limited number of more frustrating rules is presented here. Rules should be applied according to the American style of English, i.e. spelling *theater* instead of *theatre* and placing terminal marks of punctuation almost exclusively within other marks of punctuation.

Punctuation

Using terminal punctuation in relation to quotation marks

In a quoted statement that is either declarative or imperative, place the period inside the closing quotation marks.

> "The airplane crashed on the runway during takeoff."

If the quotation is followed by other words in the sentence, place a comma inside the closing quotations marks and a period at the end of the sentence.

> "The airplane crashed on the runway during takeoff," said the announcer.

In most instances in which a quoted title or expression occurs at the end of a sentence, the period is placed before either the single or double quotation marks.

> "The middle school readers were unprepared to understand Bryant's poem 'Thanatopsis.'"

> Early book-length adventure stories like *Don Quixote* and *The Three Musketeers* were known as "picaresque novels."

There is an instance in which the final quotation mark would precede the period - if the content of the sentence were about a speech or quote so that the understanding of the meaning would be confused by the placement of the period.

> The first thing out of his mouth was "Hi, I'm home."
> *but*
> The first line of his speech began "I arrived home to an empty house".

In sentences that are interrogatory or exclamatory, the question mark or exclamation point should be positioned outside the closing quotation marks if the quote itself is a statement or command or cited title.

> Who decided to lead us in the recitation of the "Pledge of Allegiance"?
>
> Why was Tillie shaking as she began her recitation, "Once upon a midnight dreary..."?
>
> I was embarrassed when Mrs. White said, "Your slip is showing"!

In sentences that are declarative but the quotation is a question or an exclamation, place the question mark or exclamation point inside the quotation marks.

> The hall monitor yelled, "Fire! Fire!"
>
> "Fire! Fire!" yelled the hall monitor.
>
> Cory shrieked, "Is there a mouse in the room?" (In this instance, the question supersedes the exclamation.)

Using periods with parentheses or brackets

Place the period inside the parentheses or brackets if they enclose a complete sentence, independent of the other sentences around it.

> Stephen Crane was a confirmed alcohol and drug addict. (He admitted as much to other journalists in Cuba.)

If the parenthetical expression is a statement inserted within another statement, the period in the enclosure is omitted.

> Mark Twain used the character Indian Joe (He also appeared in *The Adventures of Tom Sawyer*) as a foil for Jim in *The Adventures of Huckleberry Finn*.

When enclosed matter comes at the end of a sentence requiring quotation marks, place the period outside the parentheses or brackets.

"The secretary of state consulted with the ambassador [Albright]."

Using commas

Separate two or more coordinate adjectives, modifying the same word and three or more nouns, phrases, or clauses in a list.

Maggie's hair was dull, dirty, and lice-ridden.

Dickens portrayed the Artful Dodger as skillful pickpocket, loyal follower of Fagin, and defendant of Oliver Twist.

Ellen daydreamed about getting out of the rain, taking a shower, and eating a hot dinner.

In Elizabethan England, Ben Johnson wrote comedy, Christopher Marlowe wrote tragedies, and William Shakespeare composed both.

Use commas to separate antithetical or complimentary expressions from the rest of the sentence.

The veterinarian, not his assistant, would perform the delicate surgery.

The more he knew about her, the less he wished he had known.

Randy hopes to, and probably will, get an appointment to the Naval Academy.

His thorough, though esoteric, scientific research could not easily be understood by high school students.

Using double quotation marks with other punctuation

Quotations - whether words, phrases, or clauses - should be punctuated according to the rules of the grammatical function they serve in the sentence.

The works of Shakespeare, "the bard of Avon," have been contested as originating with other authors.

"You'll get my money," the old man warned, "when 'Hell freezes over'."

Sheila cited the passage that began "Four score and seven years ago...."
(Note the ellipsis followed by an enclosed period.)

"Old Ironsides" inspired the preservation of the U.S.S. Constitution. Use quotation marks to enclose the titles of shorter works: songs, short poems, short stories, essays, and chapters of books. (See "Using Italics" for punctuating longer titles.)

"The Tell-Tale Heart"   "Casey at the Bat"   "America the Beautiful"

Using semicolons

Use semicolons to separate independent clauses when the second clause is introduced by a transitional adverb. (These clauses may also be written as separate sentences, preferably by placing the adverb within the second sentence.)

The Elizabethans modified the rhyme scheme of the sonnet; thus, it was called the English sonnet.
or
The Elizabethans modified the rhyme scheme of the sonnet. It thus was called the English sonnet.

Use semicolons to separate items in a series that are long and complex or have internal punctuation.

The Italian Renaissance produced masters in the fine arts: Dante Alighieri, author of the *Divine Comedy;* Leonardo da Vinci, painter of *The Last Supper;* and Donatello, sculptor of the *Quattro Coronati*, the four saints.

The leading scorers in the WNBA were Haizhaw Zheng, averaging 23.9 points per game; Lisa Leslie, 22; and Cynthia Cooper, 19.5.

Using colons

Place a colon at the beginning of a list of items. (Note its use in the sentence about Renaissance Italians in the paragraph above.)

The teacher directed us to compare Faulkner's three symbolic novels: *Absalom, Absalom; As I Lay Dying;* and *Light in August.*

Do **not** use a comma if the list is preceded by a verb.

Three of Faulkner's symbolic novels are *Absalom, Absalom; As I Lay Dying,* and *Light in August.*

Using dashes

Place dashes to denote sudden breaks in thought.

> Some periods in literature - the Romantic Age, for example - spanned different time periods in different countries.

Use dashes instead of commas if commas are already used elsewhere in the sentence for amplification or explanation.

> The Fireside Poets included three Brahmans - James Russell Lowell, Henry David Wadsworth, Oliver Wendell Holmes - and John Greenleaf Whittier.

Use italics to punctuate the titles of long works of literature, names of periodical publications, musical scores, works of art and motion picture television, and radio programs. (When unable to write in italics, students should be instructed to underline in their own writing where italics would be appropriate.)

> *The Idylls of the King*   *Hiawatha*   *The Sound and the Fury*
> *Mary Poppins*   *Newsweek*   *The Nutcracker Suite*

Skill 2.2   Understanding various semantic elements.

Slang comes about for many reasons: Amelioration is an important one that results often in euphemisms. Examples are "passed away" for dying; "senior citizens" for old people. Some usages have become so embedded in the language that their sources are long-forgotten. For example, "fame" originally meant rumor. Some words that were originally intended as euphemisms such as "mentally retarded" and "moron" to avoid using "idiot" have themselves become pejorative.

Slang is lower in prestige than Standard English; tends to first appear in the language of groups with low status; is often taboo and unlikely to be used by people of high status; tends to displace conventional terms, either as a shorthand or as a defense against perceptions associated with the conventional term.

Informal and formal language is a distinction made on the basis of the occasion as well as the audience. At a "formal" occasion, for example, a meeting of executives or of government officials, even conversational exchanges are likely to be more formal. A cocktail party or a golf game are examples where the language is likely to be informal. Formal language uses fewer or no contractions, less slang, longer sentences, and more organization in longer segments.

Speeches delivered to executives, college professors, government officials, etc., is likely to be formal. Speeches made to fellow employees are likely to be informal. Sermons tend to be formal; Bible lessons will tend to be informal.

Jargon is a specialized vocabulary. It may be the vocabulary peculiar to a particular industry such as computers or of a field such as religion. It may also be the vocabulary of a social group. Black English is a good example. A Hardee's ad has two young men on the streets of Philadelphia discussing the merits of one of their sandwiches, and bylines are required so others may understand what they're saying. A whole vocabulary that has even developed its own dictionaries is the jargon of bloggers. The speaker must be knowledgeable about and sensitive to the jargon peculiar to the particular audience. That may require some research and some vocabulary development on the speaker's part.

Technical language is a form of jargon. It is usually specific to an industry, profession, or field of study. Sensitivity to the language familiar to the particular audience is important.

Regionalisms are those usages that are peculiar to a particular part of the country. A good example is the second person plural pronoun: you. Because the plural is the same as the singular, various parts of the country have developed their own solutions to be sure that they are understood when they are speaking to more than one "you." In the South, "you-all" or "y'all" is common. In the Northeast, one often hears "youse." In some areas of the Middlewest, "you'ns" can be heard.

Vocabulary also varies from region to region. A small stream is a "creek" in some regions but "crick" in some. In Boston, soft drinks are generically called "tonic," but it becomes "soda" in other parts of the northeast. It is "liqueur" in Canada, and "pop" when you get very far west of New York.

Semantics

To effectively teach language, it is necessary to understand that, as human beings acquire language, they realize that words have denotative and connotative meanings. Generally, denotative words point to things and connotative words deal with mental suggestions that the words convey. The word *skunk* has a denotative meaning if the speaker can point to the actual animal as he speaks the word and intends the word to identify the animal. *Skunk* has connotative meaning depending upon the tone of delivery, the socially acceptable attitudes about the animal, and the speaker's personal feelings about the animal.

Informative connotations

Informative connotations are definitions agreed upon by the society in which the learner operates. A *skunk* is "a black and white mammal of the weasel family with a pair of perineal glands which secrete a pungent odor." The *Merriam Webster Collegiate Dictionary* adds "...and offensive" odor. Identification of the color, species, and glandular characteristics are informative. The interpretation of the odor as *offensive* is affective.

Affective connotations

Affective connotations are the personal feelings a word arouses. A child who has no personal experience with a skunk and its odor or has had a pet skunk will feel differently about the word *skunk* than a child who has smelled the spray or been conditioned vicariously to associate offensiveness with the animal denoted *skunk*. The very fact that our society views a skunk as an animal to be avoided will affect the child's interpretation of the word. In fact, it is not necessary for one to have actually seen a skunk (that is, have a denotative understanding) to use the word in either connotative expression. For example, one child might call another child a skunk, connoting an unpleasant reaction (affective use) or, seeing another small black and white animal, call it a skunk based on the definition (informative use).

Using connotations

In everyday language, we attach affective meanings to words unconsciously; we exercise more conscious control of informative connotations. In the process of language development, the leaner must come not only to grasp the definitions of words but also to become more conscious of the affective connotations and how his listeners process these connotations. Gaining this conscious control over language makes it possible to use language appropriately in various situations and to evaluate its uses in literature and other forms of communication.

The manipulation of language for a variety of purposes is the goal of language instruction. Advertisers and satirists are especially conscious of the effect word choice has on their audiences. By evoking the proper responses from readers/listeners, we can prompt them to take action.

Choice of the medium through which the message is delivered to the receiver is a significant factor in controlling language. Spoken language relies as much on the gestures, facial expression, and tone of voice of the speaker as on the words he speaks. Slapstick comics can evoke laughter without speaking a word. Young children use body language overtly and older children more subtly to convey messages. These refinings of body language are paralleled by an ability to recognize and apply the nuances of spoken language. To work strictly with the written work, the writer must use words to imply the body language.

Skill 2.3   Understanding subjects relating to the analysis and history of English.

English is an Indo-European language that evolved through several periods. The origin of English dates to the settlement of the British Isles in the fifth and sixth centuries by Germanic tribes called the Angles, Saxons, and Jutes. The original Britons spoke a Celtic tongue while the Angles spoke a Germanic dialect. Modern English derives from the speech of the Anglo-Saxons who imposed not only their language but also their social customs and laws on their new land. From the fifth to the tenth century, Britain's language was the tongue we now refer to as Old English. During the next four centuries, the many French attempts at English conquest introduced many French words to English. However, the grammar and syntax of the language remained Germanic.

Middle English, most evident in the writings of Geoffrey Chaucer, dates loosely from 1066 to 1509. William Caxton brought the printing press to England in 1474 and increased literacy. Old English words required numerous inflections to indicate noun cases and plurals as well as verb conjugations. Middle English continued the use of many inflections and pronunciations that treated these inflections as separately pronounced syllables. English in 1300 would have been written "Olde Anglishe" with the *e*'s at the ends of the words pronounced as our short *a* vowel. Even adjectives had plural inflections: "long dai" became "longe daies" pronounced "long-a day-as." Spelling was phonetic, thus every vowel had multiple pronunciations, a fact that continues to affect the language.

Modern English dates from the introduction of The Great Vowels Shift because it created guidelines for spelling and pronunciation. Before the printing press, books were copied laboriously by hand; the language was subject to the individual interpretation of the scribes. Printers and subsequently lexicographers like Samuel Johnson and America's Noah Webster influenced the guidelines. As reading matter was mass produced, the reading public was forced to adopt the speech and writing habits developed by those who wrote and printed books.

Despite many students' insistence to the contrary, Shakespeare's writings are in Modern English. It is important to stress to students that language, like customs, morals, and other social factors, is constantly subject to change. Immigration, inventions and cataclysmic events change language as much as any other facet of life affected by these changes. The domination of one race or nation over others can change a language significantly. Beginning with the colonization of the New World, English and Spanish became dominant languages in the Western hemisphere. American English today is somewhat different in pronunciation and sometimes vocabulary from British English. The British call a truck a "lorry;" baby carriages a "pram," short for "perambulator;" and an elevator a "lift." There are very few syntactical differences, and even the tonal qualities that were once so clearly different are converging.

Though Modern English is less complex than Middle English, having lost many unnecessary inflections, it is still considered difficult to learn because of its many exceptions to the rules. It has, however, become the world's dominant language by reason of the great political, military, and social power of England from the fifteenth to the nineteenth century and of America in the twentieth century.

Modern inventions - the telephone, phonograph, radio, television, and motion pictures - have especially affected English pronunciation. Regional dialects, once a hindrance to clear understanding, have fewer distinct characteristics. The speakers from different parts of the United States of America can be identified by their accents, but more and more as educators and media personalities stress uniform pronunciations and proper grammar, the differences are diminishing.

The English language has a more extensive vocabulary than any other language. Ours is a language of synonyms, words borrowed from other languages, and coined words - many of them introduced by the rapid expansion of technology.

It is important for students to understand that language is in constant flux. Emphasis should be placed on learning and using language for specific purposes and audiences. Negative criticism of a student's errors in word choice or sentence structures will inhibit creativity. Positive criticism that suggests ways to enhance communication skills will encourage exploration.

Historical Events that Affected the Development of English

Perhaps the most basic principle about language in understanding its changes and variations is a simple one: language inevitably changes over time. If a community that speaks a homogeneous language and dialect are for some reason separated with no contact between the two resulting communities, over a few generations, they will be speaking different dialects and eventually will have difficulty understanding each other.

Language changes in all its manifestations: At the phonetic level, the sounds of a language will change as will its orthography. The vocabulary level will probably manifest the greatest changes. Changes in syntax are slower and less likely to occur. For example, English has changed in response to the influences of many other languages and cultures as well as internal cultural changes such as the development of the railroad and the computer; however, its syntax still relies on word order—it has not shifted to an inflected system even though many of the cultures that have impacted it do, in fact, have an inflected language, such as Spanish.

The most significant influence on a language is the blending of cultures. The Norman Conquest that brought the English speakers in the British Isles under the rule of French speakers impacted the language, but it's significant that English speakers did not adopt the language of the ruling class—they did not become speakers of French. Even so, many vocabulary items entered the language in that period. The Great Vowel Shift that occurred between the 14th and 16th centuries is somewhat of a mystery although it's generally attributed to the migration to Southeast England following the plague of the black death. The Great Vowel Shift largely accounts for the discrepancy between orthography and speech—the difficult spelling system in modern English.

Colonization of other countries has also brought new vocabulary items into the language. Indian English not only has its own easily recognizable attributes as does Australian and North American, those cultural interactions have added to items in the usages of each other and in the language at large. The fact that English is the most widely spoken and understood language all over the world in the 21st century implies that it is constantly being changed by the globalize world.

Other influences, of course, impact language. The introduction of television and its domination by the United States has had great influence on the English that is spoken and understood all over the world. The same is true of the computerizing of the world (Tom Friedman called it "flattening" in his *The World is Flat: A Brief History of the Twenty-first Century*). New terms have been added, old terms have changed meaning ("mouse," for instance), and nouns have been verbalized.

Origins of English Words

Just as countries and families have histories, so do words. Knowing and understanding the origin of a word, where it has been used down through the years, and the history of its meaning as it has changed is an important component of the writing and language teacher's tool kit. Never in the history of the English language or any other language for that matter have the forms and meanings of words changed so rapidly. When America was settled originally, immigration from many countries made it a "melting pot."

Immigration accelerated rapidly within the first hundred years, resulting in pockets of language throughout the country. When trains began to make transportation available and affordable, individuals from those various pockets came in contact with each other, shared vocabularies, and attempted to converse. From that time forward, every generation brought the introduction of a technology that made language interchange not only more possible but more important.

Radio began the trend to standardize dialects. A Bostonian might not be understood by a native of Louisiana, who might not be interested in turning the dial to hear the news or a drama or the advertisements of the vendors that had a vested interest in being heard and understood. Soap and soup producers knew a goldmine when they saw it and created a market for radio announcers and actors who spoke without a pronounced dialect. In return, listeners began to hear the English language in a dialect very different from the one they spoke, and as it settled into their thinking processes, it eventually made its way to their tongues, and spoken English began to lose some of its local peculiarities. It has been a slow process, but most Americans can easily understand other Americans, no matter where they come from. They can even converse with a native of Great Britain with little difficulty. The introduction of television carried the evolution further as did the explosion of electronic communicating devices over the past fifty years.

An excellent example of the changes that have occurred in English is a comparison of Shakespeare's original works with modern translations. Without help, twenty-first-century Americans are unable to read the *Folio*. On the other hand, teachers must constantly be mindful of the vocabularies and etymologies of their students, who are on the receiving end of the escalation brought about by technology and increased global influence and contact.

In the past, the Oxford English Dictionary has been the most reliable source for etymologies. Some of the collegiate dictionaries are also useful. *Merriam-Webster's 3rd Unabridged Dictionary* is useful in tracing the sources of words in American English. *Merriam-Webster's Unabridged Dictionary* may be out of date, so a teacher should also have a *Merriam-Webster's Collegiate Dictionary*, which is updated regularly.

However, there are many up-to-date sources for keeping up and keeping track of the changes that have occurred and are occurring constantly. Google "etymology," for instance, or even the word you're unsure of, and you can find a multitude of sources. Don't trust a single one. The information should be validated by at least three sources. Wikipedia is very useful, but it can be changed by anyone who chooses, so any information on it should be backed up by other sources. If you go to http://www.etymonline.com/sources.php, you will find a long list of resources on etymology.

In order to know when to label a usage "jargon" or "colloquial" nowadays, the teacher must be aware of the possibility that it's a word that is now accepted as standard. In order to be on top of this, the teacher must continually keep up with the etymological aids that are available, particularly online.

Spelling in English is complicated by the fact that it is not phonetic—that is, it is not based on the one-sound/one letter formula used by many other languages. The reason for this is that it is based on the Latin alphabet, which originally had twenty letters, consisting of the present English alphabet minus J, K, V, W, Y, and Z. The Romans added K to be used in abbreviations and Y and Z in words that came from the Greek. This 23-letter alphabet was adopted by the English, who developed W as a ligatured doubling of U and later J and V as consonantal variants of I and U. The result was our alphabet of 26 letters with upper case (capital) and lower case forms.

Spelling is based primarily on 15th century English. The problem is that pronunciation has changed drastically since then, especially long vowels and diphthongs. This Great Vowel Shift affected the seven long vowels. For a long time, spelling was erratic—there were no standards. As long as the meaning was clear, spelling was not considered very important. Samuel Johnson tackled this problem, and his *Dictionary of the English Language* (1755) brought standards to spelling, so important once printing presses were invented. There have been some changes, of course, through the years; but spelling is still not strictly phonetic. There have been many attempts to nudge the spelling into a more phonetic representation of the sounds, but for the most part, all have failed. A good example is Noah Webster's *Spelling Book* (1783), which was a precursor to the first edition (1828) of his *American Dictionary of the English Language*. While there are rules for spelling, and it's important that students learn the rules, there are many exceptions; and memorizing exceptions and giving plenty of opportunities for practicing them seems the only solution for the teacher of English.

COMPETENCY 3.0 COMPOSITION AND RHETORIC

Skill 3.1 Understanding strategies for teaching writing and theories of how students learn to write.

Prior to writing, you will need to prewrite for ideas and details as well as decide how the essay will be organized. In the hour you have to write you should spend no more than 5-10 minutes prewriting and organizing your ideas. As you prewrite, it might be helpful to remember you should have at least three main points and at least two to three details to support your main ideas. There are several types of graphic organizers that you should practice using as you prepare for the essay portion of the test.

PREWRITE TO EXPLAIN HOW OR WHY

Select a poem and using the visual organizer on the following page, explain how a poet creates tone and mood and uses imagery and word choice. Then complete filling out the organizer by identifying how the poet effectively creates tone and mood. Support with examples from the poem.

VISUAL ORGANIZER: GIVING REASONS

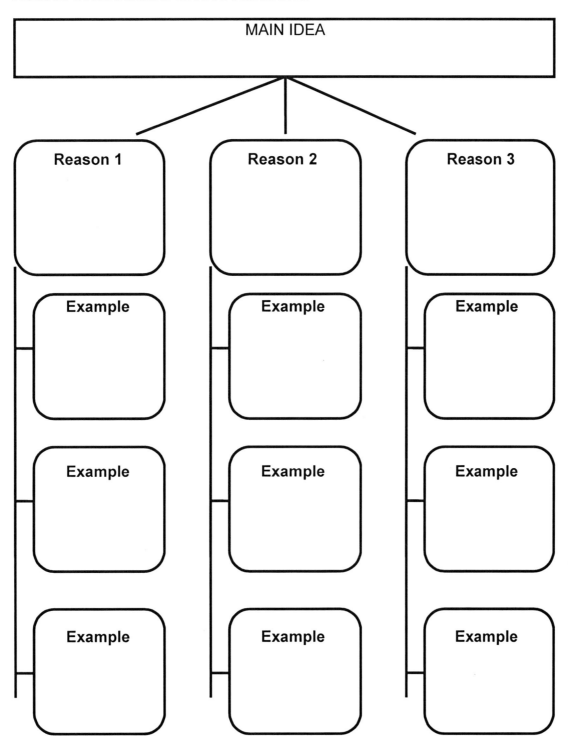

STEP 3: PREWRITE TO ORGANIZE IDEAS

After you have completed a graphic organizer, you need to decide how you will organize your essay. To organize your essay, you might consider one of the following patterns to structure your essay.

1. Examine individual elements such as **plot**, **setting**, **theme**, **character**, **point of view**, **tone**, **mood**, or **style**.

   SINGLE ELEMENT OUTLINE
   Intro - main idea statement
   Main point 1 with at least two supporting details
   Main point 2 with at least two supporting details
   Main point 3 with at least two supporting details
   Conclusion (restates main ideas and summary of main pts)

2. **Compare and contrast two elements.**

POINT-BY-POINT	BLOCK
Introduction Statement of main idea about A and B	Introduction Statement of main idea about A and B
Main Point 1 Discussion of A Discussion of B	Discussion of A Main Point 1 Main Point 2 Main point 3
Main Point 2 Discussion of A Discussion of B	Discussion of B Main Point 1 Main Point 2 Main Point 3
Main Point 3 Discussion of A Discussion of B	Conclusion Restate main idea
Conclusion Restatement or summary of main idea	

PRACTICE:
Using the cluster on the next page, choose an organizing chart and complete for your topic.

TEACHER CERTIFICATION STUDY GUIDE

VISUAL ORGANIZER: GIVING INFORMATION

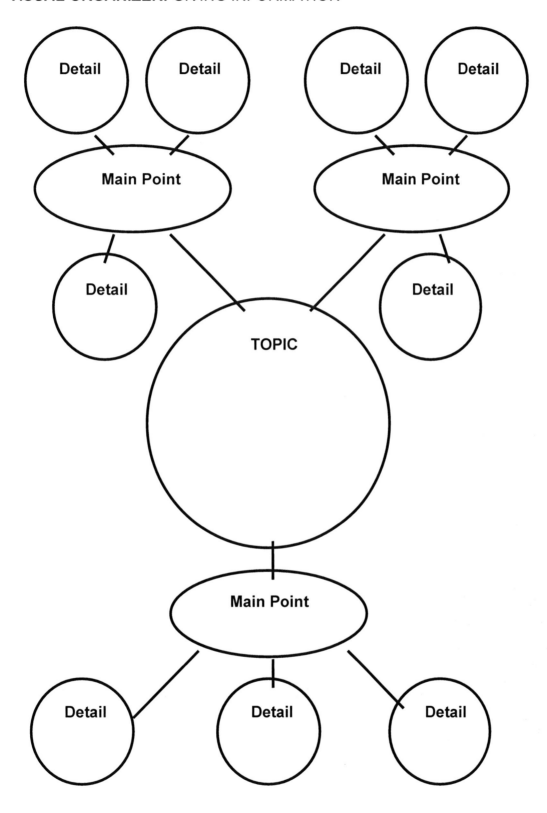

MID. SCHOOL ENG-LANG ARTS 75

Seeing writing as a process is very helpful in saving preparation time, particularly in the taking of notes and the development of drafts. Once a decision is made about the topic to be developed, some preliminary review of literature is helpful in thinking about the next step, which is to determine what the purpose of the written document will be. For example, if the topic is immigration, a cursory review of the various points of view in the debate going on in the country will help the writer decide what this particular written piece will try to accomplish. The purpose could just be a review of the various points of view, which would be an informative purpose. On the other hand, the writer might want to take a point of view and provide proof and support with the purpose of changing the reader's mind. The writer might even want the reader to take some action as the result of reading. Another possible purpose might be simply to write a description of a family of immigrants.

Once that cursory review has been completed, it's time to begin research in earnest and to prepare to take notes. If the thesis has been clearly defined, and some thought has been given to what will be used to prove or support it, a tentative outline can be developed. A thesis plus three points is typical. Decisions about introduction and conclusion should be deferred until the body of the paper is written. Note-taking is much more effective if the notes are being taken to provide information for an outline. There is much less danger that the writer will go off on time-consuming tangents.

Formal outlines inhibit effective writing. However, a loosely constructed outline can be an effective device for note-taking that will yield the information for a worthwhile statement about a topic. Sentence outlines are better than topic outlines because they require the writer to do some thinking about the direction a subtopic will take.

Once this preliminary note-taking phase is over, the first draft can be developed. The writing at this stage is likely to be highly individualistic. However, successful writers tend to just write, keeping in mind the purpose of the paper, the point that is going to be made in it, and the information that has been turned up in the research. Student writers need to understand that this first draft is just that—the first one. It takes more than one draft to write a worthwhile statement about a topic. This is what successful writers do. It's sometimes helpful to have students read the various drafts of a story by a well-known writer.

Once the draft is on paper, a stage that is sometimes called editing occurs. With word processors, this is much more easily achieved than in the past. Sections can be deleted, words can be changed, and additions can be made without doing the entire project over a second time.

What to look for: mechanics, of course, spelling, punctuation, etc., but it's important that student writers not mistake that for editing. Editing is rereading objectively, testing the effectiveness on a reader of the arrangement and the line of reasoning. The kinds of changes that will need to be made are: rearranging the parts, adding information that is missing and needed and deleting information that doesn't fit or contribute to the accomplishment of the purpose.

Once the body of the paper has been shaped to the writer's satisfaction, the introduction and conclusion should be fashioned. An introduction should grab the reader's interest and, perhaps, announce the purpose and thesis of the paper unless the reasoning is inductive, in which case, purpose and thesis may come later in the paper. The conclusion is to reaffirm the purpose in some way.

Enhancing Interest:
- Start out with an attention-grabbing introduction. This sets an engaging tone for the entire piece and will be more likely to pull the reader in.
- Use dynamic vocabulary and varied sentence beginnings. Keep the reader on their toes. If they can predict what you are going to say next, switch it up.
- Avoid using clichés (as cold as ice, the best thing since sliced bread, nip it in the bud). These are easy shortcuts, but they are not interesting, memorable, or convincing.

Ensuring Understanding:
- Avoid using the words, "clearly," "obviously," and "undoubtedly." Often, things that are clear or obvious to the author are not as apparent to the reader. Instead of using these words, make your point so strongly that it is clear on its own.
- Use the word that best fits the meaning you intend, even if it is longer or a little less common. Try to find a balance, a go with a familiar yet precise word.
- When in doubt, explain further.

Techniques to Maintain Focus:
- **Focus on a main point.** The point should be clear to readers, and all sentences in the paragraph should relate to it.
- **Start the paragraph with a topic sentence.** This should be a general, one-sentence summary of the paragraph's main point, relating both back towards the thesis and toward the content of the paragraph. (A topic sentence is sometimes unnecessary if the paragraph continues a developing idea clearly introduced in a preceding paragraph, or if the paragraph appears in a narrative of events where generalizations might interrupt the flow of the story.)
- **Stick to the point.** Eliminate sentences that do not support the topic sentence.

Be flexible. If there is not enough evidence to support the claim your topic sentence is making, do not fall into the trap of wandering or introducing new ideas within the paragraph. Either find more evidence, or adjust the topic sentence to collaborate with the evidence that is available.

Stories

It seems simplistic, yet it's an often-overlooked truism: the first and most important measure of a story is the story itself. *The story's the thing.* However, a good story must have certain characteristics. Without conflict there is no story, so determining what the conflicts are should be a priority for the writer. Once the conflicts are determined, the outcome of the story must be decided. Who wins? Who loses? And what factors go into making one side of the equation win out over the other one? The pattern of the plot is also an important consideration. Where is the climax going to occur? Is denouement necessary? Does the reader need to see the unwinding of all the strands? Many stories fail because a denouement is needed but not supplied.

Characterization, the choice the writer makes about the devices he/she will use to reveal character, requires an understanding of human nature and the artistic skill to convey a personality to the reader. This is usually accomplished subtly through dialogue, interior monologue, description, and the character's actions and behavior. In some successful stories, the writer comes right out and tells the reader what this character is like. However, sometimes there will be discrepancies between what the narrator tells the reader about the character and what is revealed to be actual, in which case the narrator is unreliable, and that unreliability of the voice the reader must depend on becomes an important and significant device for understanding the story.

Point of view is a powerful tool not only for the writer but for the enjoyment and understanding of the reader. The writer must choose among several possibilities: first-person narrator objective, first-person narrator omniscient, third-person objective, third-person omniscient, and third-person limited omniscient. The most successful story-writers use point of view very creatively to accomplish their purposes. If a writer wishes to be successful, he/she must develop point-of-view skills.

Style—the unique way a writer uses language—is often the writer's signature. The reader does not need to be told that William Faulkner wrote a story to know it because his style is so distinctive that it is immediately recognizable. Even the writing of Toni Morrison, which could be said to be Faulknerian, cannot be mistaken for the work of Faulkner, himself.

The writer must be cognizant of his/her own strengths and weaknesses and continually work to hone the way sentences are written, words are chosen, and descriptions are crafted until they are razor-sharp. The best advice to the aspiring writer: read the works of successful writers. If a writer wants to write a best-seller, then that writer needs to be reading best-sellers.

Poetry

Writing poetry in the 21st century is quite a different thing from writing it in earlier periods. There was a time when a poem was required to fit a certain pattern or scheme. Poetry was once defined as a piece of writing that was made up of end-rhymes. No more. The rhymed poem makes up only a small percentage of worthwhile and successful poems nowadays.

The first skill to work on for the budding poet is descriptive writing, defined as language that appeals to one or more of the five senses. A good poem makes it possible for the reader to experience an emotional event—seeing a mountain range as the sun dawns, watching small children on a playground, smelling the fragrance of a rose, hearing a carillon peal a religious tune at sunset, feeling fine silk under one's fingers. Creating language that makes that experience available to the readers is only the first step, however, because the ultimate goal is to evoke an emotional response. Feeling the horror of the battleground, weeping with the mother whose child was drowned, exulting with a winning soccer team. It's not enough to tell the reader what it's like. It's the *showing* that is necessary.

The aspiring poet should know the possibilities as well as the limitations of this genre. A poem can tell a story, for instance, but the emotional response is more important than the story itself. Edgar Allen Poe, in an 1842 review of Hawthorne's *Twice-Told Tales* in *Graham's Magazine* had important advice for the writer of poetry: " . . . the unity of effect or impression is a point of the greatest importance." Even though he considered the tale or short story the best way to achieve this, he wrote several memorable poems and much of his prose writing is considered to be as close to poetry as to prose by most critics. He also wrote in 1847, in an expansion of his critique of Hawthorne's works, that ". . .true originality . . .is that which, in bringing out the half-formed, the reluctant, or the unexpressed fancies of mankind, or in exciting the more delicate pulses of the heart's passion, or in giving birth to some universal sentiment or instinct in embryo, thus combines with the pleasurable effect of *apparent* novelty, a real egoistic delight."

Play writing

Play writing uses many of the same skills that are necessary to successful story writing. However, in addition to those skills, there are many more required of the writer who wishes his/her story to be told on stage or on film. The point of view, of course, is always objective unless the writers uses the Shakespearean device of the soliloquy, where a player steps forward and gives information about what's going on. The audience must figure out the meaning of the play on the basis of the actions and speeches of the actors.

A successful playwright is expert in characterization as described above under

Story.

What a character is like is determined by dialogue, appearance (costume, etc.), behavior, actions. A successful playwright also understands motivation. If a character's behavior cannot be traced to motivating circumstances, the audience will probably find the action incoherent—a major barrier to positive reception of the play.

The writing must be very carefully honed. Absolutely no excess of words can be found in a successful play. It takes very little time to lose an audience; every word counts. The playwright should concentrate on saying the most possible with the fewest words possible.

Setting is an important feature of the play. Most plays have only one because changing settings in the middle is difficult and disrupting. This calls for a very special kind of writing. The entire action of the play must either take place within the setting or be brought forth in that setting by the reporting or recounting of what is going on outside of the setting by one or more of the characters. The writer must determine what the setting will be. The actual building and creation of the set is in the hands of another kind of artist—one who specializes in settings.

The plot of most plays is rising; that is, the conflicts are introduced early in the play and continue to develop and intensify over the life of the play. As a general rule, the climax is the last thing that happens before the final curtain falls, but not necessarily. Plots of plays demonstrate the same breadth of patterns that are true of stories. For example, a play may end with nothing resolved. Denouement is less likely to follow a climax in a play than in a story, but epilogues do sometimes occur.

Writing Voice

There are at least thirteen possible choices for point of view (voice) in literature as demonstrated and explained by Wallace Hildick in his *13 Types of Narrative* (London: MacMillan and Co., 1968). However, for purposes of helping students write essays about literature, three, or possibly four, are adequate. The importance of teaching students to use this aspect of a piece of literature to write about it is not just as an analytic exercise but also should help them think about how a writer's choices impact the overall effect of the work.

Point of view or voice is essentially through whose eyes the reader sees the action. The most common is the third-person objective. If the story is seen from this point of view, the reader watches the action, hears the dialogue, reads descriptions and from all of those must deduce characterization—what sort of person a character is. In this point of view, an unseen narrator tells the reader what is happening, using the third person, he, she, it, they. The effect of this point of view is usually a feeling of distance from the plot.

More responsibility is on the reader to make judgments than in other points of view. However, the author may intrude and evaluate or comment on the characters or the action.

The voice of the first-person narrator is often used also. The reader sees the action through the eyes of an actor in the story who is also telling the story. In writing about a story that uses this voice, the narrator must be analyzed as a character. What sort of person is this? What is this character's position in the story—observer, commentator, actor? Can the narrator be believed, or is he/she biased? The value of this voice is that, while the reader is able to follow the narrator around and see what is happening through that character's eyes, the reader is also able to feel what the narrator feels. For this reason, the writer can involve the reader more intensely in the story itself and move the reader by invoking feelings—pity, sorrow, anger, hate, confusion, disgust, etc. Many of the most memorable novels are written in this point of view.

Another voice often used may best be titled "omniscient" because the reader is able to get into the mind of more than one character or sometimes all the characters. This point of view can also bring greater involvement of the reader in the story. By knowing what a character is thinking and feeling, the reader is able to empathize when a character feels great pain and sorrow, which tends to make a work memorable. On the other hand, knowing what a character is thinking makes it possible to get into the mind of a pathological murderer and may elicit horror or disgust.

"Omniscient" can be broken down into third-person omniscient or first-person omniscient. In third-person omniscient, the narrator is not seen or known or acting in the story but is able to watch and record not only what is happening or being said, but what characters are thinking. In first-person omniscient on the other hand, the narrator plays a role in the story but can also record what other characters are thinking. It is possible, of course, that the narrator is the pathological murderer, which creates an effect quite different than a story where the thoughts of the murderer are known but the narrator is standing back and reporting his behavior, thoughts, and intents.

Point of view or voice is a powerful tool in the hands of a skillful writer. The questions to be answered in writing an essay about a literary work are: What point of view has this author used? What effect does it have on the story? If it had been written in a different voice, how would the story be different?

Most credible literary works are consistent in point of view but not always, so consistency is another aspect that should be analyzed. Does the point of view change? Where does it vary? Does it help or hurt the effect of the story?

Skill 3.2   Recognizing individual and collaborative approaches to teaching writing.

Viewing writing as a process allows teachers and students to see the writing classroom as a cooperative workshop where students and teachers encourage and support each other in each writing endeavor. Listed below are some techniques that help teachers to facilitate and create a supportive classroom environment.

1. Create peer response/support groups that are working on similar writing assignments. The members help each other in all stages of the writing process-from prewriting, writing, revising, editing, and publishing.

2. Provide several prompts to give students the freedom to write on a topic of their own. Writing should be generated out of personal experience and students should be introduced to in-class journals. One effective way to get into writing is to let them write often and freely about their own lives, without having to worry about grades or evaluation.

3. Respond in the form of a question whenever possible. Teacher/facilitator should respond noncritically and use positive, supportive language.

4. Respond to formal writing acknowledging the student's strengths and focusing on the composition skills demonstrated by the writing. A response should encourage the student by offering praise for what the student has done well. Give the student a focus for revision and demonstrate that the process of revision has applications in many other writing situations.

5. Provide students with readers' checklists so that students can write observational critiques of others' drafts, and then they can revise their own papers at home using the checklists as a guide.

6. Pair students so that they can give and receive responses. Pairing students keeps them aware of the role of an audience in the composing process and in evaluating stylistic effects.

7. Focus critical comments on aspects of the writing that can be observed in the writing. Comments like "I noticed you use the word 'is' frequently" will be more helpful than "Your introduction is dull" and will not demoralize the writer.

8. Provide the group with a series of questions to guide them through the group writing sessions.

Multimedia refers to a technology for presenting material in both visual and verbal forms. This format is especially conducive to the classroom, since it reaches both visual and auditory learners.

Knowing how to select effective teaching software is the first step in efficient multi-media education. First, decide what you need the software for (creating spreadsheets, making diagrams, creating slideshows, etc.) Consult magazines such as *Popular Computing, PC World, MacWorld,* and *Multimedia World* to learn about the newest programs available. Go to a local computer store and ask a customer service representative to help you find the exact equipment you need. If possible, test the programs you are interested in. Check reviews in magazines such as *Consumer Reports, PCWorld, Electronic Learning* or *MultiMedia Schools* to ensure the software's quality.

Software programs useful for producing teaching material
- Adobe PageMaker, PhotoShop, and Acrobat
- Aldus Freehand
- CorelDRAW!
- DrawPerfect
- Claris Works
- PC Paintbrush
- Harvard Graphics
- Visio
- Microsoft Word
- Microsoft Power Point

In learning to write and in improving one's writing, the most useful exercise is editing/revising. Extensive revision is the hallmark of most successful writers. In the past, writers, student writers in particular, have been reluctant to revise because it meant beginning over to prepare the document for final presentation.

However, that time is long gone. The writing of graduate dissertations took on a whole new dimension after the creation of the word processor and before long, classroom writing teachers were able to use this function to help students improve their writing.

Requiring extensive revision in writing classrooms nowadays is not unreasonable and can be an important stage in the production of papers. Microsoft Word has had a "tracking" capability in its last several upgrades, which carries revision a step further. Now the teacher and student can carry on a dialogue on the paper itself. The teacher's deletions and additions can be tracked, the student can respond, and the tracking will be facilitated by automatically putting the changes in a different color. The "comment" function makes it possible for both teacher and student to write notes at the exactly relevant point in the manuscript.

Skill 3.3   Knowledge of various tools and response strategies for assessing student writing.

When assessing and responding to student writing, there are several guidelines to remember.

Responding to non-graded writing (formative).

1. Avoid using a red pen. Whenever possible use a #2 pencil.
2. Explain the criteria that will be used for assessment in advance.
3. Read the writing once while asking the question, "Is the student's response appropriate for the assignment?"
4. Reread and make note at the end whether the student met the objective of the writing task.
5. Responses should be non-critical and use supportive and encouraging language.
6. Resist writing on or over the student's writing.
7. Highlight the ideas you wish to emphasize, question, or verify.
8. Encourage your students to take risks.

Responding to and evaluating graded writing (summative).

1. Ask students to submit prewriting and rough-draft materials including all revisions with their final draft.
2. For the first reading, use a holistic method, examining the work as a whole.
3. When reading the draft for the second time, assess it using the standards previously established.
4. Responses to the writing should be written in the margin and should use supportive language.

5. Make sure you address the process as well as the product. It is important that students value the learning process as well as the final product.
6. After scanning the piece a third time, write final comments at the end of the draft.

Sometimes this exercise is seen by students as simply catching errors in spelling or word use. Students need to reframe their thinking about revising and editing. Some questions that need to be asked:

- Is the reasoning coherent?
- Is the point established?
- Does the introduction make the reader want to read this discourse?
- What is the thesis? Is it proven?
- What is the purpose? Is it clear? Is it useful, valuable, interesting?
- Is the style of writing so wordy that it exhausts the reader and interferes with engagement?
- Is the writing so spare that it is boring?
- Are the sentences too uniform in structure?
- Are there too many simple sentences?
- Are too many of the complex sentences the same structure?
- Are the compounds truly compounds or are they unbalanced?
- Are parallel structures truly parallel?
- If there are characters, are they believable?
- If there is dialogue, is it natural or stilted?
- Is the title appropriate?
- Does the writing show creativity or is it boring?
- Is the language appropriate? Is it too formal? Too informal? If jargon is used, is it appropriate?

Studies have clearly demonstrated that the most fertile area in teaching writing is this one. If students can learn to revise their own work effectively, they are well on their way to becoming effective, mature writers. Word processing is an important tool for teaching this stage in the writing process. Microsoft Word has tracking features that make the revision exchanges between teachers and students more effective than ever before.

- Have students write a short story, essay or other specified genre of writing
- Assess their ability to write about a given body of knowledge in a logical and critical way
- Observe their ability to use language resources appropriate for the required task.
- Use a rating system. For example, a scale from 1 to 4 (where 1=unsatisfactory and 4=excellent).
- Monitor their use of source material

- Evaluate the structure and development of their writing
- Ensure that their writing style is appropriate for the task assigned
- Check for grammatical correctness
- Provide follow-up support for any weaknesses detected

Skill 3.4   Recognizing, understanding, and evaluating rhetorical features of writing and organizational strategies.

Organizational Structures

Authors use a particular organization to best present the concepts which they are writing about. Teaching students to recognize organizational structures helps them to understand authors' literary intentions, and helps them in deciding which structure to use in their own writing.

Cause and Effect: When writing about *why* things happen, as well as *what* happens, authors commonly use the cause and effect structure. For example, when writing about how he became so successful, a CEO might talk about how he excelled in math in high school, moved to New York after college, and stuck to his goals even after multiple failures. These are all *causes* that lead to the *effect*, or result, of him becoming a wealthy and powerful businessman.

Compare and Contrast: When examining the merits of multiple concepts or products, compare and contrast lends itself easily to organization of ideas. For example, a person writing about foreign policy in different countries will put them against each other to point out differences and similarities, easily highlighting the concepts the author wishes to emphasize.

Problem and Solution: This structure is used in a lot of handbooks and manuals. Anything organized around procedure-oriented tasks, such as a computer repair manual, gravitates toward a problem and solution format, because it offers such clear, sequential text organization.

An easy and effective way of organizing information to be used in a work of nonfiction is by asking specific questions that are geared towards a particular mode of presentation. An example of these questions follows:

Useful research questions:

What is it?

It is the process of thinking up and writing down a set of questions that you want to answer about the research topic you have selected.

Why should I do it?

It will keep you from getting lost or off-track when looking for information. You will try to find the answers to these questions when you do your research.

When do I do it?

After you have written your statement of purpose, and have a focused topic to ask questions about, begin research.

How do I do it?

Make two lists of questions. Label one "factual" questions and one "interpretive" questions. The answers to factual questions will give your reader the basic background information they need to understand your topic. The answers to interpretive questions show your creative thinking in your project and can become the basis for your thesis statement.

Asking factual questions:

Assume your reader knows nothing about your subject. Make an effort to tell them everything they need to know to understand what you will say in your project.

Make a list of specific questions that ask: Who? What? When? Where?

Example: For a report about President Abraham Lincoln's attitude and policies towards slavery, people will have to know; Who was Abraham Lincoln? Where and when was he born? What political party did he belong to? When was he elected president? What were the attitudes and laws about slavery during his lifetime? How did his actions affect slavery?

Asking Interpretive Questions:

These kinds of questions are the result of your own original thinking. They can be based on the preliminary research you have done on your chosen topic. Select one or two questions to answer in your presentation. They can be the basis of forming a thesis statement.

- **Hypothetical**: How would things be different today if something in the past had been different?

Example: How would our lives be different today if the Confederate (southern) states had won the United States Civil War? What would have happened to the course of World War Two if the Atomic Bomb hadn't been dropped on Hiroshima and Nagasaki?

- **Prediction**: How will something look or be in the future, based on the way it is now?

Example: What will happen to sea levels if global warming due to ozone layer depletion continues and the polar caps melt significantly? If the population of China continues to grow at the current rate for the next fifty years, how will that impact its role in world politics?

- **Solution**: What solutions can be offered to a problem that exists today?

Example: How could global warming be stopped? What can be done to stop the spread of sexually transmitted diseases among teenagers?

- **Comparison or Analogy**: Find the similarities and differences between your main subject and a similar subject, or with another subject in the same time period or place.

Example: In what ways is the Civil War in the former Yugoslavia similar to (or different from) the United States Civil War?
What is the difference in performance between a Porsche and a Lamborghini?

- **Judgment**: Based on the information you find, what can you say as your informed opinion about the subject?

Example: How does tobacco advertising affect teen cigarette smoking? What are the major causes of eating disorders among young women? How does teen parenthood affect the future lives of young women and men?

Introductions:

It's important to remember that in the writing process, the introduction should be written last. Until the body of the paper has been determined—thesis, development—it's difficult to make strategic decisions regarding the introduction. The Greek rhetoricians called this part of a discourse *exordium*, a "leading into." The basic purpose of the introduction, then, is to lead the audience into the discourse. It can let the reader know what the purpose of the discourse is and it can condition the audience to be receptive to what the writer wants to say. It can be very brief or it can take up a large percentage of the total word count. Aristotle said that the introduction could be compared to the flourishes that flute players make before their performance—an overture in which the musicians display what they can play best in order to gain the favor and attention of the audience for the main performance.

In order to do this, we must first of all know what we are going to say; who the readership is likely to be; what the social, political, economic, etc., climate is; what preconceived notions the audience is likely to have regarding the subject; and how long the discourse is going to be.

There are many ways to do this:
- Show that the subject is important.
- Show that although the points we are presenting may seem improbable, they are true.
- Show that the subject has been neglected, misunderstood, or misrepresented.
- Explain an unusual mode of development.
- Forestall any misconception of the purpose.
- Apologize for a deficiency.
- Arouse interest in the subject with an anecdotal lead-in.
- Ingratiate oneself with the readership.
- Establish one's own credibility.

The introduction often ends with the thesis, the point or purpose of the paper. However, this is not set in stone. The thesis may open the body of the discussion, or it may conclude the discourse. The most important thing to remember is that the purpose and structure of the introduction should be deliberate if it is to serve the purpose of "leading the reader into the discussion."

Conclusions:

It's easier to write a conclusion after the decisions regarding the introduction have been made. Aristotle taught that the conclusion should strive to do five things:

1. Inspire the reader with a favorable opinion of the writer.
2. Amplify the force of the points made in the body of the paper.
3. Reinforce the points made in the body.
4. Rouse appropriate emotions in the reader.
5. Restate in a summary way what has been said.

The conclusion may be short or it may be long depending on its purpose in the paper. Recapitulation, a brief restatement of the main points or certainly of the thesis is the most common form of effective conclusions. A good example is the closing argument in a court trial.

Text Organization:

In studies of professional writers and how they produce their successful works, it has been revealed that writing is a process that can be clearly defined although in practice it must have enough flexibility to allow for creativity. The teacher must be able to define the various stages that a successful writer goes through in order to make a statement that has value. There must be a discovery stage when ideas, materials, supporting details, etc., are deliberately collected. These may come from many possible sources: the writer's own experience and observations, deliberate research of written sources, interviews of live persons, television presentations, or the internet.

The next stage is organization where the purpose, thesis, and supporting points are determined. Most writers will put forth more than one possible thesis and in the next stage, the writing of the paper, settle on one as the result of trial and error. Once the paper is written, the editing stage is necessary and is probably the most important stage. This is not just the polishing stage. At this point, decisions must be made regarding whether the reasoning is cohesive—does it hold together? Is the arrangement the best possible one or should the points be rearranged? Are there holes that need to be filled in? What form will the introduction take? Does the conclusion lead the reader out of the discourse or is it inadequate or too abrupt, etc.

It's important to remember that the best writers engage in all of these stages recursively. They may go back to discovery at any point in the process. They may go back and rethink the organization, etc. To help students become effective writers, the teacher needs to give them adequate practice in the various stages and encourage them to engage deliberately in the creative thinking that makes writers successful.

Short Essays

COMPETENCY 4.0 LITERARY ANALYSIS

Stimulus

The stimulus for the literary analysis question will consist of a selection of prose (fiction or nonfiction) **OR** poetry (a whole short poem or an excerpt from a longer work).

Skill 4.1   **Describe and give examples of the use of one or two specified literary element(s) present in the stimulus.**

See Skill 1.3.

Skill 4.2   **Discuss how the author's use of the literary element(s) contributes to the overall meaning and/or effectiveness of the text.**

Writing about an author's use of plot should begin with determining what the conflicts are. In a naturalist story, the conflicts may be between the protagonist and a hostile or indifferent world. Sometimes, the conflicts are between two characters, the protagonist and the antagonist; and sometimes the conflicts are internal—between two forces within an individual character that have created a dilemma. For example, a Catholic priest may be devoted and committed to his role in the Church that calls for a celibate life yet at the same time be deeply in love with a woman.

Once the conflicts have been determined, the pattern of action will hinge on how the story comes out. Who (or what) wins and who (or what) loses. If the protagonist struggles throughout the story but emerges triumphant in the end, the pattern is said to be rising. On the other hand, if the story is about the downfall of the major character, the story can be said to be falling. If there is no winner in the end, the pattern is flat. This is an important point for a writer to make because it is crucial to all other aspects of an analysis of a work of fiction.

Characters are developed in many ways. Sometimes the writer simply tells the reader what kind of person this is. More often, however, the reader is left to deduce the characteristics from dialogue with others; with what other characters think or say about him/her; with description—what the character looks like, tall, short, thin, plump, dark-haired, gray-haired, etc. The techniques a writer uses to define character are called characterization, and a writer will usually deal with these matters when writing an analysis.

Setting can be a period of time, the 1930s, for example. It can also be a place, either a real place like a particular city or a fictional place like a farm or a mansion.

It can be emotional—some of Truman Capote's stories are set in an atmosphere of fear and danger, and the effectiveness of the story depends on that setting. An analysis should deal with the *function* of the setting in the story. For example, if it is set in a particular period of time as *The Great Gatsby* is, would it be a different story if it were set in a different period of time? A setting can sometimes function as a symbol, so the writer should be looking for that as a possibility.

Theme in a work of fiction is similar to a thesis in an essay. It's the *point* the story makes. In a story, it may possibly be spoken by one of the characters; but more often, it is left to the writer to determine. This requires careful reading and should take into account the other aspects of the story before a firm decision is made with regard to the point of the story. Different analysts will come to different conclusions about what a story means. Very often the thesis of an analytical essay will be the writer's declaration of the theme according to his/her own well-reasoned opinion.

Point of view seems simple on the surface, but it rarely is in a story. In fact, Wallace Hildick wrote *Thirteen Types of Narrative* to explain point of view in literature. The most common ones are first person narrator objective in which the person telling the story only records his/her observations of what is happening. In this point of view, the only clues as to what the characters are like come from the narrator. The attitude of the narrator toward the theme or the characters will be an important part of the story and should be dealt with in an analysis. Sometimes, its' apparent that the narrator's view does not square with reality, in which the narrator becomes unreliable and the reader must make an effort to determine what is real and what is not. If a writer uses this device, it's extremely important that the analyst point it out and point out what it does for the story.

The first person narrator may know what one or more of the characters is thinking and that will be important to the analysis of the story. If the narrator knows this, how did he/she acquire the knowledge? The most logical way is that the story was told to the narrator in the first place by that character or those characters.

Third person objective is another common form of development. In this point of view, there is no narrator. The story is told by an unseen observer. The reader does not know what anyone is thinking, only what is being said and described.

Third person omniscient is also fairly common. In this point of view, the story is being told by an unseen observer, but the observer is able to know what at least one person is thinking, which is sometimes called limited omniscient point of view. The reader may also know what most or all of the characters are thinking, and this point of view is simply called third-person omniscient.
Point of view is extremely powerful in the way a story is perceived and must be dealt with in a written analysis.

COMPETENCY 5.0 RHETORICAL ANALYSIS

Stimulus

The stimulus for the rhetorical analysis question will consist of a selection of fiction or nonfiction prose.

Skill 5.1 Identify and describe and/or give examples of the use of one or more rhetorical elements in the stimulus.

A logical argument consists of three stages. First of all, the propositions which are necessary for the argument to continue are stated. These are called the premises of the argument. They are the evidence or reasons for accepting the argument and its conclusions.

Premises (or assertions) are often indicated by phrases such as "because", "since", "obviously" and so on. (The phrase "obviously" is often viewed with suspicion, as it can be used to intimidate others into accepting suspicious premises. If something doesn't seem obvious to you, don't be afraid to question it. You can always say "Oh, yes, you're right, it is obvious" when you've heard the explanation.)

Next, the premises are used to derive further propositions by a process known as inference. In inference, one proposition is arrived at on the basis of one or more other propositions already accepted. There are various forms of valid inference.

The propositions arrived at by inference may then be used in further inference. Inference is often denoted by phrases such as "implies that" or "therefore".

Finally, we arrive at the conclusion of the argument -- the proposition which is affirmed on the basis of the premises and inference. Conclusions are often indicated by phrases such as "therefore", "it follows that", "we conclude" and so on. The conclusion is often stated as the final stage of inference.

Classical Argument

In its simplest form, the classical argument has five main parts:

The **introduction**, which warms up the audience, establishes goodwill and rapport with the readers, and announces the general theme or thesis of the argument.

The **narration**, which summarizes relevant background material, provides any information the audience needs to know about the environment and circumstances that produce the argument, and set up the stakes—what's at risk in this question.

The **confirmation** lays out, in a logical order (usually strongest to weakest or most obvious to most subtle), the claims that support the thesis, providing evidence for each claim.

The **refutation and concession**, which looks at opposing viewpoints to the writer's claims, anticipating objections from the audience, and allowing as much of the opposing viewpoints as possible without weakening the thesis.

The **summation**, which provides a strong conclusion, amplifying the force of the argument, shows the readers that this solution is the best at meeting the circumstances.

Skill 5.2   **Discuss the degree to which the use of the rhetorical element(s) is effective in conveying the author's point and contributing to the overall meaning of the text.**

In studies of professional writers and how they produce their successful works, it has been revealed that writing is a process that can be clearly defined although in practice it must have enough flexibility to allow for creativity. The teacher must be able to define the various stages that a successful writer goes through in order to make a statement that has value. There must be a discovery stage when ideas, materials, supporting details, etc., are deliberately collected. These may come from many possible sources: the writer's own experience and observations, deliberate research of written sources, interviews of live persons, television presentations, or the internet.

The next stage is organization where the purpose, thesis, and supporting points are determined. Most writers will put forth more than one possible thesis and in the next stage, the writing of the paper, settle on one as the result of trial and error. Once the paper is written, the editing stage is necessary and is probably the most important stage. This is not just the polishing stage. At this point, decisions must be made regarding whether the reasoning is cohesive—does it hold together? Is the arrangement the best possible one or should the points be rearranged? Are there holes that need to be filled in? What form will the introduction take? Does the conclusion lead the reader out of the discourse or is it inadequate or too abrupt, etc.

It's important to remember that the best writers engage in all of these stages recursively. They may go back to discovery at any point in the process. They may go back and rethink the organization, etc. To help students become effective writers, the teacher needs to give them adequate practice in the various stages and encourage them to engage deliberately in the creative thinking that makes writers successful.

Sample Test

Essay Question

Read the passage below from *The Diary of Anne Frank* (1947); then complete the exercise that follows.

Written on July 15, 1944, three weeks before the Frank family was arrested by the Nazis, Anne's diary entry explains her worldview and future hopes.

"It's difficult in times like these: ideals, dreams and cherished hopes rise within us, only to be crushed by grim reality. It's a wonder I haven't abandoned all my ideals, they seem so absurd and impractical. Yet I cling to them because I still believe, in spite of everything, that people are truly good at heart.

"It's utterly impossible for me to build my life on a foundation of chaos, suffering and death. I see the world being slowly transformed into a wilderness, I hear the approaching thunder that, one day, will destroy us too, I feel the suffering of millions, And yet, when I look up at the sky, I somehow feel that everything will change for the better, that this cruelty too shall end, that peace and tranquility will return once more. In the meantime, I must hold on to my ideals. Perhaps the day will come when I will be able to realize them!"

Using your knowledge of literature, write a response in which you:

- Compare and contrast Anne's ideals with her awareness of the conditions in which she lives; and
- Discuss how the structure of Anne's writing—her sentences and paragraphs—emphasize the above contrast.

Sample Weak Response

Anne Frank's ideals in this writing make readers clear on the point that she was strongly against Hitler and the Nazis. You can tell that she knows the Nazis are very dangerous and violent people who cause "the suffering of millions." Otherwise, why would she have written this? This fact of Nazis causing the suffering of millions of people, and killing them, is a large contrast to how much she believes "that people are truly good at heart." Anne Frank is right about her ideals. And that is why her whole book is such a large contrast to the conditions in which she lived in WWII, when everything was going wrong in the world. You can also tell from this passage that she is a lot smarter than Hitler was. That is another big contrast in the book.

Anne's sentences and paragraphs emphasize the above contrast. They are not fiction; they are her own real thoughts, and these thoughts don't cause "a grim reality" of "cruelty" or the "absurd and impractical" things that she talks about as the war's fault. No, Anne's words cause us to see what is true and real in her art and in her heart. She makes us see that love is not the fiction. Hitler and the Nazis are the ones who make the fiction. We can read this in between the lines, which sometimes have to be done.

Back when Anne Frank wrote her words down on paper, everything was going wrong around her but she knew what to do, and she did it. She wrote a world classic story about her life. This story is a big contrast to what the Germans were doing.

Sample Strong Response

This excerpt from *The Diary of Anne Frank* reveals the inner strength of a young girl who refuses, despite the wartime violence and danger surrounding her, to let her idealism be overcome by hatred and mass killing. This idealism is reflected, in part, by her emphases on universal human hopes such as peace, tranquility, and goodwill. But Anne Frank is no dreamy Pollyanna. Reflecting on her idealism in the context of the war raging around her, she matter-of-factly writes: "my dreams, they seem so absurd and impractical."

This indicates Anne Frank's awareness of not only her own predicament but of human miseries that extend beyond the immediate circumstances of her life. For elsewhere she writes in a similar vein, "In times like these… I see the world being slowly transformed into a wilderness"; despite her own suffering she can "feel the suffering of millions."

And yet Anne Frank believes, "in spite of everything, that people are truly good at heart." This statement epitomizes the stark existential contrast of her worldview with the wartime reality that ultimately claimed her life.

The statement also exemplifies how Anne's literary form—her syntax and diction—mirror thematic content and contrasts. "In spite of everything," she still believes in people. She can "hear the approaching thunder…yet, when I look up at the sky, I somehow feel that everything will change for the better." At numerous points in this diary entry, first-hand knowledge of violent tragedy stands side-by-side with belief in humanity and human progress.

"I must hold on to my ideals," Anne concludes. "Perhaps the day will come when I'll be able to realize them!" In her diary she has done so, and more.

Multiple-Choice Questions

1. Children's literature became established in the (Easy) (Skill 1.1)

   A. seventeenth century
   B. eighteenth century
   C. nineteenth century
   D. twentieth century

2. Which of the following would be the most significant factor in teaching Homer's *Iliad* and *Odyssey* to any particular group of students? (Rigorous) (Skill 1.1)

   A. Identifying a translation on the appropriate reading level
   B. Determining the students' interest level
   C. Selecting an appropriate evaluative technique
   D. Determining the scope and delivery methods of background study

3. Written on the sixth grade reading level, most of S. E. Hinton's novels (for instance, *The Outsiders*) have the greatest reader appeal with (Easy) (Skill 1.1)

   A. sixth graders.
   B. ninth graders.
   C. twelfth graders.
   D. adults.

4. Which of the following is the most effective strategy for motivating reluctant readers to read more? (Rigorous) (Skill 1.1)

   A. providing the readers with a variety of books
   B. making reading time enjoyable
   C. requiring a set amount of reading per day
   D. including reading as part of the grade

5. After watching a movie of a train derailment, a child exclaims, "Wow, look how many cars fell off the tracks. There's junk everywhere. The engineer must have really been asleep." Using the facts that the child is impressed by the wreckage and assigns blame to the engineer, a follower of Piaget's theories would estimate the child to be about (Rigorous) (Skill 1.1)

   A. ten years old.
   B. twelve years old.
   C. fourteen years old.
   D. sixteen years old.

6. *Diction* is best defined as (Average) (Skill 1.2)

   A. The specific word choices an author makes in order to create a particular mood or feeling in the reader.
   B. Writing that explains something thoroughly.
   C. The background, or exposition, for a short story or drama.
   D. Word choices that help teach a truth or moral.

7. What is the best course of action when a child refuses to complete an assignment on the grounds that it is morally objectionable? (Rigorous) (Skill 1.2)

   A. Speak with the parents and explain the necessity of studying this work.
   B. Encourage the child to sample some of the text before making a judgment.
   C. Place the child in another teacher's class where students are studying an acceptable work.
   D. Provide the student with alternative material that serves the same curricular purpose.

8. Which of the following responses to literature typically give middle school students the most problems? (Average) (Skill 1.2)

   A. Interpretive
   B. Evaluative
   C. Critical
   D. Emotional

9. A figure of speech in which someone absent or something inhuman is addressed as though present and able to respond describes (Easy) (Skill 1.3)

   A. personification.
   B. synechdoche.
   C. metonymy.
   D. apostrophe.

10. The appearance of a Yankee from Connecticut in the Court of King Arthur is an example of a/an (Easy) (Skill 1.3)

    A. rhetoric.
    B. parody.
    C. paradox.
    D. anachronism.

11. "Clean as a whistle" and "easy as falling off a log" exemplify (Average) (Skill 1.3)

    A. semantics.
    B. parody.
    C. irony.
    D. clichés.

12. The literary device of personification is used in which example below? (Average)) (Skill 1.3)

    A. "Beg me no beggary by soul or parents, whining dog!"
    B. "Happiness sped through the halls cajoling as it went."
    C. "O wind thy horn, thou proud fellow."
    D. "And that one talent which is death to hide."

13. Which of the following terms does *not* denote a figure of speech (figurative language)? (Easy) (Skill 1.3)

    A. Simile
    B. Euphemism
    C. Onomatopoeia
    D. Allusion

14. Consider the following poem:

    My name is John Welington Wells,
    I'm a dealer in magic and spells,
    In blessings and curses,
    And ever-fill'd purses,
    In prophecies, witches, and knells. (Easy) (Skill 1.4)

    A. sonnet
    B. haiku
    C. limerick
    D. cinquain

15. Which of the following is not a theme of Native American writing? (Average) (Skill1.5)

    A. Emphasis on the hardiness of the human body and soul
    B. The strength of multi-cultural assimilation
    C. Indignation about the genocide of native peoples
    D. Remorse for the loss of the Indian way of life

16. The principal writer of *The Declaration of Independence* was (Average) (Skill 1.5)

    A. Patrick Henry
    B. Thomas Jefferson
    C. Ben Franklin
    D. George Washington

17. Pearl appears as an important character in (Average) (Skill 1.5)

    A. *The Scarlet Letter*
    B. *Moby Dick*
    C. *The House of the Seven Gables*
    D. "The Cask of Amontillado"

18. The first African American to receive the Pulitzer Prize for Poetry was (Average) (Skill 1.5)

    A. Gwendolyn Brooks
    B. Harriet E. Wilson
    C. Richard Wright
    D. James Edwin Campbell

19. Which item below is not a research-based strategy that supports reading? (Rigorous) (Skill 1.6)

    A. reading more
    B. reading along with a more proficient reader
    C. reading a passage no more than twice
    D. self-monitoring progress

20. Use the table below to answer the question that follows it.

	Math Usage	General Usage
bi (two)	bilinear bimodal binomial	bicycle biplane bifocals
cent (100)	centimeter centigram percent	century centigrade centipede
circum (around)	circumference circumradius circumcenter	circumnavigate circumstance Circumspect

Which vocabulary strategy does the table above exemplify? (Rigorous) (Skill 1.6)

    A. Frayer method
    B. morphemic analysis
    C. semantic mapping
    D. word mapping

21. A teacher has taught his students to self-monitor their reading by locating where in the passage they are having difficulty, identifying the specific problem there, and restating the difficult sentence or passage in their own words. These strategies are examples of (Average) (Skill 1.6)

    A. graphic and semantic organizers
    B. metacognition
    C. recognizing story structure
    D. summarizing

22. Regularly requiring students to practice reading short, instructional-level texts at least three times to a peer and to give and receive peer feedback about these readings mainly addresses which reading skill? (Average) (Skill 1.6)

    A. Comprehension
    B. fluency
    C. evaluation
    D. word-solving

23. For students with poor vocabularies, the teacher should recommend first that (Rigorous) (Skill 1.6)

   A. they enroll in a Latin class.
   B. they read newspapers, magazines and books on a regular basis.
   C. they write the words repetitively after looking them up in the dictionary.
   D. they use a thesaurus to locate and incorporate the synonyms found there into their vocabularies.

24. Before reading a passage, a teacher gives her students an anticipation guide with a list of statements related to the topic they are about to cover in the reading material. She asks the students to indicate their agreement or disagreement with each statement on the guide. This activity is intended to (Rigorous) (Skill 1.6)

   A. elicit students' prior knowledge of the topic and set a purpose for reading
   B. help students to identify the main ideas and supporting details in the text
   C. help students to synthesize information from the text
   D. help students to visualize the concepts and terms in the text

25. Among junior-high school students of low-to-average readability levels which work would most likely stir reading interest? (Rigorous) (Skill 1.6)

   A. *Elmer Gantry*, Sinclair Lewis
   B. *Smiley's People*, John LeCarre
   C. *The Outsiders*, S. E. Hinton
   D. *And Then There Were None*, Agatha Christie

26. Students are fluent readers if they (Rigorous) (Skill 1.6)

   A. read texts with expression or prosody.
   B. read word-to-word and haltingly.
   C. must intentionally decode a majority of the words.
   D. write disorganized sentences

27. Reading assessment should take place (Rigorous) (Skill 1.6)

   A. At the end of the semester.
   B. At the end of a unit.
   C. Constantly.
   D. All of the above.

28. Which of the following approaches is *not* useful in assessing slower or immature readers? (Rigorous) (Skill 1.6)

    A. Repeated readings.
    B. Echo reading.
    C. Wide reading.
    D. Reading content that is more difficult than their skill levels in order to "stretch" their abilities.

29. Middle-School students bring little, if any, initial experience in (Rigorous) (Skill 1.6)

    A. Phonics.
    B. Phonemics.
    C. Textbook reading assignments.
    D. Stories read by the teacher.

30. Middle-School students bring little, if any, initial experience in (Rigorous) (Skill 1.6)

    A. Phonics.
    B. Phonemics.
    C. Textbook reading assignments.
    D. Stories read by the teacher.

31. To enhance reading comprehension, experts recommend all of these techniques *except for* (Rigorous) (Skill 1.6)

    A. Read material through only once, but read slowly and carefully.
    B. Read material through more than once according to a plan.
    C. Create a map for the next reading.
    D. Highlight or take notes during reading.

32. The most significant drawback to applying learning theory research to classroom practice is that (Rigorous) (Skill 1.6)

    A. today's students do not acquire reading skills with the same alacrity as when greater emphasis was placed on reading classical literature.
    B. development rates are complicated by geographical and cultural differences that are difficult to overcome.
    C. homogeneous grouping has contributed to faster development of some age groups.
    D. social and environmental conditions have contributed to an escalated maturity level than research done twenty or more years ago would seem to indicate.

33. The students in Mrs. Cline's seventh grade language arts class were invited to attend a performance of *Romeo and Juliet* presented by the drama class at the high school. To best prepare, they should (Rigorous) (Skill 1.6)

    A. read the play as a homework exercise.
    B. read a synopsis of the plot and a biographical sketch of the author.
    C. examine a few main selections from the play to become familiar with the language and style of the author.
    D. read a condensed version of the story and practice attentive listening skills.

34. Which aspect of language is innate? (Average) (Skill 1.6)

    A. Biological capability to articulate sounds understood by other humans
    B. Cognitive ability to create syntactical structures
    C. Capacity for using semantics to convey meaning in a social environment
    D. Ability to vary inflections and accents

35. Which of the following reading strategies calls for higher order cognitive skills? (Rigorous) (Skill 1.6)

    A. making predictions
    B. summarizing
    C. skimming
    D. making inferences

36. The most effective strategy for learning vocabulary is (Rigorous) (Skill 1.6)

    A. memorizing lists
    B. guessing from context
    C. finding words in the dictionary
    D. researching the word's history

37. Which of the following bits of information best describes the structure of English? (Average) (Skill 2.1)

    A. Syntax based on word order
    B. Inflected
    C. Romantic
    D. Orthography is phonetic

38. Which of the following sentences contains an error in agreement? (Easy) (Skill 2.1)

    A. Jennifer is one of the women who writes for the magazine.
    B. Each one of their sons plays a different sport.
    C. This band has performed at the Odeum many times.
    D. The data are available online at the listed website.

39. Which group of words is not a sentence? (Easy) (Skill 2.1)

   A. In keeping with the graduation tradition, the students, in spite of the rain, standing in the cafeteria tossing their mortarboards.
   B. Rosa Parks, who refused to give up her seat on the bus, will be forever remembered for her courage.
   C. Taking advantage of the goalie's being out of the net, we scored our last and winning goal.
   D. When it began to rain, we gathered our possessions and ran for the pavilion.

40. Identify the sentence that has an error in parallel structure. (Easy) (Skill 2.1)

   A. In order to help your favorite cause, you should contribute time or money, raise awareness, and write congressmen.
   B. Many people envision scientists working alone in a laboratory and discovering scientific breakthroughs.
   C. Some students prefer watching videos to textbooks because they are used to visual presentation.
   D. Tom Hanks, who has won two Academy Awards, is celebrated as an actor, director, and producer.

41. Which of the following sentences is unambiguously properly punctuated? (Average) (Skill 2.1)

   A. The more you eat; the more you want.
   B. The authors—John Steinbeck, Ernest Hemingway, and William Faulkner—are staples of modern writing in American literature textbooks.
   C. Handling a wild horse, takes a great deal of skill and patience.
   D. The man, who replaced our teacher, is a comedian.

42. A punctuation mark indicating omission, interrupted thought, or an incomplete statement is a/an (Average) (Skill 2.1)

   A. ellipsis.
   B. anachronism.
   C. colloquy.
   D. idiom.

43. Which of the following contains an error in possessive punctuation? (Easy) (Skill 2.1)

   A. Doris's shawl
   B. mother's-in-law frown
   C. children's lunches
   D. ambassador's briefcase

44. Which level of meaning is the hardest aspect of a language to master? (Rigorous) (Skill 2.2)

    A. denotation
    B. jargon
    C. connotation
    D. slang

45. This statement, "I'll die if I don't pass this course," exemplifies a/an: (Easy) (Skill 2.2)

    A. barbarism.
    B. oxymoron.
    C. hyperbole.
    D. antithesis.

46. Read the following passage:

    "It would have been hard to find a passer-by more wretched in appearance. He was a man of middle height, stout and hardy, in the strength of maturity; he might have been forty-six or seven. A slouched leather cap hid half his face, bronzed by the sun and wind, and dripping with sweat."

    What is its main form of discourse? (Easy) (Skill 2.2)

    A. Description
    B. Narration
    C. Exposition
    D. Persuasion

47. Consider the following sentence:

    Mr. Brown is a school volunteer <u>with a reputation and twenty years</u> <u>service</u>.

    Which phrase below best represents the logical intent of the underlined phrase above (Choice E is identical to the underlined phrase). (Rigorous) (Skill 2.2)

    A. with a reputation for twenty years' service
    B. with a reputation for twenty year's service
    C. who has served twenty years
    D. with a service reputation of twenty years

48. Consider the following sentence:

    Joe <u>didn't hardly know his cousin Fred</u>, who'd had a rhinoplasty.

    Which word group below best conveys the intended meaning of the underlined section above? (Average) (Skill 2.2)

    A. hardly did know his cousin Fred
    B. didn't know his cousin Fred hardly
    C. hardly knew his cousin Fred
    D. didn't know his cousin Fred

49. The substitution of "went to his rest" for "died" exemplifies a/an (Easy) (Skill 2.2)

    A. bowdlerism.
    B. jargon.
    C. euphemism.
    D. malapropism.

50. The arrangement and relationship of words in sentences or sentence structures best describes (Average) (Skill 2.2)

    A. style.
    B. discourse.
    C. thesis.
    D. syntax.

51. Which aspect of language shows the most evident change over time? (Average) (Skill 2.3)

    A. phonetics
    B. vocabulary
    C. syntax
    D. spelling

52. The Old English period refers to (Average) (Skill 2.3)

    A. The Fourth Century
    B. The Third through the Eighth Century
    C. The Fifth through the Tenth Century
    D. The Fifth through the Eighth Century

53. What factor below introduced Modern English? (Rigorous) (Skill 2.3)

    A. The Great Vowel Shift
    B. The printing press
    C. The invasion of the Normans
    D. Phonetic spelling

54. Which of the following is not true about English? (Rigorous) (Skill 2.3)

    A. English is the easiest language to learn.
    B. English is the least inflected language.
    C. English has the most extensive vocabulary of any language.
    D. English originated as a Germanic tongue.

55. If a student uses slang and expletives, what is the best course of action to take in order to improve the student's formal communication skills? (Rigorous) (Skill 3.1)

   A. ask the student to rephrase their writing; that is, translate it into language appropriate for the school principal to read.
   B. refuse to read the student's papers until he conforms to a more literate style.
   C. ask the student to read his work aloud to the class for peer evaluation.
   D. rewrite the flagrant passages to show the student the right form of expression.

56. Oral debate is most closely associated with which form of discourse? (Average) (Skill 3.1)

   A. Description
   B. Exposition
   C. Narration
   D. Persuasion

57. A composition with no voice will lack the following quality (Rigorous) (Skill 3.1)

   A. organization
   B. appeal
   C. illustrations
   D. ideas

58. A conversation between two or more people is called a/an: (Easy) (Skill 3.1)

   A. parody.
   B. dialogue.
   C. monologue.
   D. analogy.

59. To explain or to inform belongs in the category of (Average) (Skill 3.1)

   A. exposition.
   B. narration.
   C. persuasion.
   D. description.

60. Varying the complexity of a graphic organizer exemplifies differentiating which aspect of a lesson? (Rigorous) (Skill 3.1)

   A. its content/topic
   B. its environment
   C. its process
   D. its product

61. Modeling is a practice that requires students to (Average) (Skill 3.1)

   A. create a style unique to their own language capabilities.
   B. emulate the writing of professionals.
   C. paraphrase passages from good literature.
   D. peer evaluate the writings of other students.

62. In a timed essay test of an hour's duration, how much time should be devoted to prewriting. (Easy) (Skill 3.1)

    A. five
    B. ten
    C. fifteen
    D. twenty

63. A student informative composition should consist of a minimum of how many paragraphs? (Easy) (Skill 3.1)

    A. three
    B. four
    C. five
    D. six

64. Which of the following is the least effective procedure for promoting consciousness of audience? (Rigorous) (Skill 3.1)

    A. Pairing students during the writing process
    B. Reading all rough drafts before the students write the final copies
    C. Having students compose stories or articles for publication in school literary magazines or newspapers
    D. Writing letters to friends or relatives

65. Which of the following is not a technique of prewriting? (Average) (Skill 3.1)

    A. Clustering
    B. Listing
    C. Brainstorming
    D. Proofreading

66. Writing ideas quickly without interruption of the flow of thoughts or attention to conventions is called (Easy) (Skill 3.1)

    A. brainstorming.
    B. mapping.
    C. listing.
    D. Free writing.

67. Computer-assisted instruction (CAI) accommodates all of the following factors in reading instruction *except for* (Average) (Skill 3.2)

    A. free-form responses to comprehension questions
    B. increased motivation
    C. the addition of speech with computer-presented text
    D. the use of computers for word processing, and the integration of writing instruction with reading

68. Which of the four underlined sections of the following sentence contains an error that a word processing spellchecker probably wouldn't catch? (Rigorous) (Skill 3.2)

    He tuc the hors by the rains and pulled it back to the stabel.

    A. tuc
    B. hors
    C. rains
    D. stabel

69. In the hierarchy of needs for adolescents who are becoming more team-oriented in their approach to learning, which need do they exhibit most? (Rigorous) (Skill 3.2)

   A. Need for competence
   B. Need for love/acceptance
   C. Need to know
   D. Need to belong

70. Overcrowded classes prevent the individual attention needed to facilitate language development. This drawback can be best overcome by (Rigorous) (Skill 3.2)

   A. Dividing the class into independent study groups.
   B. Assigning more study time at home.
   C. Using more drill practice in class.
   D. Team teaching.

71. All of the following techniques are used to observe student progress (conduct ongoing informal assessment) except for (Average) (Skill 3.3)

   A. analyzing the student work product at key stages
   B. collecting data from assessment tests
   C. posing strategic questions
   D. observing students as they work

72. Effective assessment requires that (Rigorous) (Skill 3.3)

   A. Students not be involved in the assessment process.
   B. Testing activities are kept separate from the teaching activities.
   C. It assesses what classroom instruction has prepared the student to read.
   D. Tests, in order to be reliable, should never use materials previously studied in the classroom

73. Effective assessment means that (Rigorous) (Skill 3.3)

   A. It ignores age and cultural considerations
   B. Students' weaknesses are emphasized.
   C. Only reading skills count.
   D. It is integrated with instruction and is not intrusive.

74. Reading a piece of student writing to assess the overall impression of the product is (Easy) (Skill 3.3)

   A. holistic evaluation.
   B. portfolio assessment.
   C. analytical evaluation.
   D. using a performance system.

75. A formative evaluation of student writing (Easy) (Skill 3.3)

   A. requires a thorough marking of mechanical errors with a pencil or pen.
   B. makes comments on the appropriateness of the student's interpretation of the prompt and the degree to which the objective was met.
   C. requires the student to hand in all the materials produced during the process of writing.
   D. involves several careful readings of the text for content, mechanics, spelling, and usage.

76. What type of comprehension do questions beginnings with "who," "what," "where," or "how" assess? (Average) (Skill 3.4)

   A. evaluative
   B. inferential
   C. literal
   D. narrative

77. A paper explaining the relationship between food and weight gain contains the signal words "because," "consequently," "this is how," and "due to." These words suggest that the paper has which text structure? (Average) (Skill 3.4)

   A. cause and effect structure
   B. compare and contrast structure
   C. descriptive structure
   D. sequential structure

78. A paper written in first person and having characters, a setting, a plot, some dialogue, and events sequenced chronologically with some flashbacks exemplifies which genre? (Average) (Skill 3.4)

   A. exposition
   B. narration
   C. persuasion
   D. speculation

79. In 'inverted triangle' introductory paragraphs, the thesis sentence occurs (Easy) (Skill 3.4)

   A. at the beginning of the paragraph.
   B. in the middle of the paragraph.
   C. at the end of the paragraph.
   D. in the second paragraph.

80. Which of the following should not be included in the opening paragraph of an informative essay? (Average) (Skill 3.4)

   A. Thesis sentence
   B. Details and examples supporting the main idea
   C. broad general introduction to the topic
   D. A style and tone that grabs the reader's attention

Answer Key

1. A	38. A
2. A	39. A
3. B	40. C
4. B	41. B
5. A	42. A
6. A	43. B
7. D	44. C
8. B	45. C
9. D	46. A
10. D	47. D
11. D	48. C
12. B	49. C
13. C	50. D
14. C	51. B
15. B	52. C
16. B	53. A
17. A	54. A
18. A	55. A
19. C	56. D
20. B	57. B
21. C	58. B
22. B	59. A
23. B	60. C
24. A	61. B
25. C	62. B
26. A	63. C
27. D	64. B
28. D	65. D
29. D	66. D
30. C	67. A
31. A	68. C
32. D	69. B
33. D	70. A
34. A	71. B
35. D	72. C
36. B	73. D
37. A	74. A
	75. B
	76. C
	77. A
	78. B
	79. C
	80. B

Rigor Table

	Easy %20	Average Rigor %40	Rigorous %40
Question #	1, 3, 9, 10, 13, 14, 38, 39, 40, 43, 45, 46, 49, 58, 62, 63, 66, 74, 75, 79	6, 8, 11, 12, 15, 16, 17, 18, 21, 22, 34, 37, 41, 42, 48, 50, 51, 52, 56, 59, 61, 65, 67, 71, 76, 77, 78, 80	2, 4, 5, 7, 19, 20, 23, 24, 25, 26, 27, 28, 29, 30, 31, 32, 33, 35, 36, 44, 47, 53, 54, 55, 57, 60, 64, 68, 69, 70, 72, 73

TEACHER CERTIFICATION STUDY GUIDE

Rationales with Sample Questions

1. Children's literature became established in the (Skill 1.1) (Easy)

    A. seventeenth century
    B. eighteenth century
    C. nineteenth century
    D. twentieth century

The answer is A. In the seventeenth century, Jean de la Fontaine's *Fables*, Pierre Perreault's *Tales*, Mme. d'Aulnoye's novels based on old folktales, and Mme. de Beaumont's *Beauty and the Beast* created a children's literature genre. In England, Perreault was translated, and a work allegedly written by Oliver Smith, *The Renowned History of Little Goody Two Shoes*, helped to establish children's literature in England, too.

2. Which of the following would be the most significant factor in teaching Homer's *Iliad* and *Odyssey* to any particular group of students? (Skill 1.1) (Rigorous)

    A. Identifying a translation on the appropriate reading level
    B. Determining the student's interest level
    C. Selecting an appropriate evaluative technique
    D. Determining the scope and delivery methods of background study

The answer is A. Students will appreciate these two works if the translation reflects both the vocabulary they know and their reading level. Choice B is moot because most students aren't initially interested in Homer. Choice C skips to later matters. Choice D is tempting and significant, but not as crucial as having an accessible text.

3. Written on the sixth grade reading level, most of S. E. Hinton's novels (for instance, *The Outsiders*) have the greatest reader appeal with (Skill 1.1) (Easy)

    A. sixth graders.
    B. ninth graders.
    C. twelfth graders.
    D. adults.

The answer is B. Adolescents are concerned with their changing bodies, their relationships with each other and adults, and their place in society. Reading *The Outsiders* helps them confront different problems that they are only now beginning to experience as teenagers, such as gangs and social identity. The book is universal in its appeal to adolescents.

4. Which of the following is the most effective strategy for motivating reluctant readers to read more? (Skill 1.1) (Rigorous)

    A. providing the readers with a variety of books
    B. making reading time enjoyable
    C. requiring a set amount of reading per day
    D. including reading as part of the grade

The answer is B. The key to motivating students to read is to foster a love of reading. Making sure that reading time is an enjoyable time that students look forward to will certainly be an incentive for reluctant readers.

5. After watching a movie of a train derailment, a child exclaims, "Wow, look how many cars fell off the tracks. There's junk everywhere. The engineer must have really been asleep." Using the facts that the child is impressed by the wreckage and assigns blame to the engineer, a follower of Piaget's theories would estimate the child to be about (Skill 1.1) (Rigorous)

    A. ten years old.
    B. twelve years old.
    C. fourteen years old.
    D. sixteen years old.

The answer is A. According to Piaget's theory, children seven to eleven years old begin to apply logic to concrete things and experiences. They can combine performance and reasoning to solve problems. They have internalized moral values and are willing to confront rules and adult authority.

6. *Diction* is best defined as (Skill 1.2)(Average)

    A. The specific word choices an author makes in order to create a particular mood or feeling in the reader.
    B. Writing that explains something thoroughly.
    C. The background, or exposition, for a short story or drama.
    D. Word choices that help teach a truth or moral.

The answer is A. Diction refers to an author's choice of words, expressions and style to convey his/her meaning. The other choices are only marginally related to this meaning, so the choice is a clear one.

MID. SCHOOL ENG-LANG ARTS

7. What is the best course of action when a child refuses to complete an assignment on the ground that is morally objectionable? (Skill 1.2) (Rigorous)

   A. Speak with the parents and explain the necessity of studying this work.
   B. Encourage the child to sample some of the text before making a judgment.
   C. Place the child in another teacher's class where students are studying an acceptable work.
   D. Provide the student with alternative material that serves the same curricular purpose.

The answer is D. This approach is the most time efficient and flexible. Choice A requires conversations involving value systems that aren't going to change. Choice B risks being open to the charge of exposing children to controversial material despite parental input. Choice C is a disproportionate disruption to the student's schedule and the school routine.

8. Which of the following responses to literature typically give middle school students the most problems? (Skill 1.2) (Average)

   A. Interpretive
   B. Evaluative
   C. Critical
   D. Emotional

The answer is B. Middle school readers will exhibit both emotional and interpretive responses. In middle/junior high school, organized study models enable students to identify main ideas and supporting details, to recognize sequential order, to distinguish fact from opinion, and to determine cause/effect relationships. Middle school students can provide reasons to support their assertions that a particular book was boring or a particular poem made him or her feel sad, and this is to provide a critical reaction on a fundamental level. Evaluative responses, however, require students to address how the piece represents its genre, how well it reflects the social and ethical mores of a given society, or how well the author has employed a fresh approach to the subject. Evaluative responses are more sophisticated than critical responses, and they are appropriate for advanced high school students.

9. A figure of speech in which someone absent or something inhuman is addressed as though present and able to respond describes (Skill 1.3) (Easy)

   A. personification.
   B. synechdoche.
   C. metonymy
   D. apostrophe.

The answer is D. An apostrophe differs from a personification in the important respect that a "someone" cannot be "personified," plus personifications come in far more varieties than are suggested by the definition in question. A synechdoche is a figure of speech which represents some whole or group by one of its or their parts or members. Metonymy is the substitution of a word for a related word.

10. The appearance of a Yankee from Connecticut in the Court of King Arthur is an example of a/an (Skill 1.3) (Easy)

    A. rhetoric.
    B. parody.
    C. paradox.
    D. anachronism.

The answer is D. Anachronism is the placing of characters, persons, events or things into time frames incongruent with their actual dates. Parody is poking fun at something. Paradox is a seeming contradiction. Anachronism is something out of time frame.

11. "Clean as a whistle" and "easy as falling off a log" exemplify (Skill 1.3) (Average)

    A. semantics.
    B. parody.
    C. irony.
    D. clichés.

The answer is D. A cliché is a phrase or expression that has become dull due to overuse. Semantics is a field of language study. Parody is poking fun at something. Irony is using language to create an unexpected or opposite meaning of the literal words being used.

TEACHER CERTIFICATION STUDY GUIDE

12. **The literary device of personification is used in which example below? (Skill 1.3) (Average)**

    A. "Beg me no beggary by soul or parents, whining dog!"
    B. "Happiness sped through the halls cajoling as it went."
    C. "O wind thy horn, thou proud fellow."
    D. "And that one talent which is death to hide."

The correct answer is B. Personification is defined as giving human characteristics to inanimate objects or concepts. It can be thought of as a sub-category of metaphor. Happiness, an abstract concept, is "speeding through the halls" and "cajoling," both of which are human behaviors, so Happiness is being compared to a human being. Choice A is figurative and metaphorical, but not a personification. Choice C is, again, figurative and metaphorical, but not a personification. The speaker is, perhaps, telling someone that they are bragging, or "blowing their own horn." Choice D is also figurative and metaphorical, but not personification. Hiding a particular talent is being compared to risking death.

13. **The substitution of "went to his rest" for "died" exemplifies a/an (Skill 1.3) (Easy)**

    A. bowdlerism.
    B. jargon.
    C. euphemism.
    D. malapropism.

The answer is C. A euphemism alludes to a distasteful topic in a pleasant manner in order to obscure or soften the disturbing impact of the original. A bowdlerism is a prudish version of something. Jargon is language specific to some occupation or activity. A Malapropism is the improper use of a word that sounds like the word that would fit the context. The result is most often ludicrous.

MID. SCHOOL ENG-LANG ARTS

14. **Consider the following poem:**

   My name is John Welington Wells,
   I'm a dealer in magic and spells,
   In blessings and curses,
   And ever-fill'd purses,
   In prophecies, witches, and knells. (Skill 1.4) (Easy)

   A. sonnet
   B. haiku
   C. limerick
   D. cinquain

The correct answer is C. A limerick is a five line, humorous verse, often nonsensical. with a rhyme scheme of aabba . Lines 1, 2, and 5 usually have eight syllables each; and lines 3 and 4 have five syllables. Line 5 is often some type of 'zinger.' A sonnet is a 14-line poem in iambic pentameter and having a definite rhyme scheme. Shakespearean and Petrarchan sonnets are the main varieties. A cinquain is a five-line poem with one word in line 1, two words in line 2, and so on through line 5.

15. **Which of the following is not a theme of Native American writing? (Skill 1.5) (Average)**

   A. Emphasis on the hardiness of the human body and soul
   B. The strength of multi-cultural assimilation
   C. Indignation about the genocide of native peoples
   D. Remorse for the loss of the Indian way of life

The answer is B. Originating in a vast body of oral traditions from as early as before the fifteenth century, Native American literature themes include "nature as sacred," "the interconnectedness of life," "the hardiness of body and soul," "indignation about the destruction of the Native American way of life," and "the genocide of many tribes by the encroaching settlements of European Americans." These themes are still present in today's Native American literature, such as in the works of Duane Niatum, Gunn Allen, Louise Erdrich and N. Scott Momaday.

16. The principal writer of *The Declaration of Independence* was (Skill 1.5) (Average)

   A. Patrick Henry
   B. Thomas Jefferson
   C. Ben Franklin
   D. George Washington

The correct answer is B. Thomas Jefferson. Although Benjamin Franklin was responsible for editing it and making it the prime example of neoclassical writing that it is, *The Declaration of Independence* came directly from the mind and pen of Jefferson. Patrick Henry was a great orator, and his speeches played an important role in precipitating the revolution. Although George Washington's *Farewell to the Army of the Potomac* is an important piece of writing from that era, he was not the principal writer of the declaration.

17. Pearl appears as an important character in (Skill 1.5) (Average)

   A. The Scarlet Letter
   B. Moby Dick
   C. The House of the Seven Gables
   D. "The Cask of Amontillado"

The correct answer is A. Pearl is the illegitimate daughter of Hester Prynne in Nathaniel Hawthorne's *The Scarlet Letter*. *Moby Dick* is Herman Melville's great opus about the pursuit of a great white whale. *The House of the Seven Gables*, like *The Scarlet Letter,* is about a society that promulgates loneliness and suspicion. "The Cask of Amontillado" is one of Poe's horror stories.

18. The first African American to receive the Pulitzer Prize for Poetry was (Skill 1.5) (Average)

   A. Gwendolyn Brooks
   B. Harriet E. Wilson
   C. Richard Wright
   D. James Edwin Campbell

The correct answer is A. Gwendolyn Brooks was the first African American to receive the Pulitzer Prize for Poetry. Harriett E. Wilson, who died in 1900, was the first female African American novelist. Richard Wright was a novelist and black activist. James Edwin Campbell was a 19th century African American poet, editor, writer, and educator.

19. Which item below is not a research-based strategy that supports reading? (Skill 1.6) (Rigorous)

    A. reading more
    B. reading along with a more proficient reader
    C. reading a passage no more than twice
    D. self-monitoring progress

The correct answer is C. Actually, research shows that reading a passage several times improves fluency, and, depending on the complexity of the material, improves comprehension, too. The more complex the material, the more comprehension value in repeated readings.

20. Use the table below to answer the question that follows it.

	Math Usage	General Usage
bi (two)	bilinear	bicycle
	bimodal	biplane
	binomial	bifocals
cent (100)	centimeter	century
	centigram	centigrade
	percent	centipede
circum (around)	circumference	circumnavigate
	circumradius	circumstance
	circumcenter	Circumspect

Which vocabulary strategy does the table above exemplify? (Skill 1.6) (Rigorous)

    A. Frayer method
    B. morphemic analysis
    C. semantic mapping
    D. word mapping

The answer is B. Morphemes are the smallest units of language that have an associated meaning. The purpose of morphemic analysis is to apply morphemic awareness to the task of learning new words. The Frayer method involves having students use their own words to define new words and to link those definitions to personal experiences. Semantic mapping incorporates graphical clues to concepts and is a subset of graphic organizers. Word mapping is another subset of graphic organizers and consists of displaying such information as the various forms a word may take as it transforms through the parts of speech.

21. A teacher has taught his students to self-monitor their reading by locating where in the passage they are having difficulty, by identifying the specific problem there, and by restating the difficult sentence or passage in their own words. These strategies are examples of (Skill 1.6) (Average)

    A. graphic and semantic organizers
    B. metacognition
    C. recognizing story structure
    D. summarizing

The correct answer is C. Good readers use metacognitive strategies (various ways of thinking about thinking) to improve their reading. Before reading, they clarify their purpose for reading and preview the text. During reading, they monitor their understanding, adjusting their reading speed to fit the difficulty of the text and fixing any comprehension problems they have. After reading, they check their understanding of what they read.

22. Regularly requiring students to practice reading short, instructional-level texts at least three times to a peer and to give and receive peer feedback about these readings mainly addresses which reading skill? (Skill 1.6) (Average)

    A. Comprehension
    B. fluency
    C. evaluation
    D. word-solving

The correct answer is B. Fluency is the ability to read text quickly with accuracy, phrasing, and expression. Fluency develops over time and requires substantial reading practice. This activity provides just this sort of practice. The peer feedback portion does address comprehension, evaluation, and some word-solving; but the main thrust is on fluency development.

23. For students with poor vocabularies, the teacher should recommend first that (Skill 1.6) (Rigorous)

    A. they enroll in a Latin class.
    B. they read newspapers, magazines and books on a regular basis.
    C. they write the words repetitively after looking them up in the dictionary.
    D. they use a thesaurus to locate and incorporate the synonyms found there into their vocabularies.

The answer is B. Regularly reading a wide variety of materials for pleasure and information is the best way to develop a stronger vocabulary. The other suggestions have limited application and do not serve to reinforce an enthusiasm for reading.

24. Before reading a passage, a teacher gives her students an anticipation guide with a list of statements related to the topic they are about to cover in the reading material. She asks the students to indicate their agreement or disagreement with each statement on the guide. This activity is intended to (Skill 1.6) (Rigorous)

    A. elicit students' prior knowledge of the topic and set a purpose for reading
    B. help students to identify the main ideas and supporting details in the text
    C. help students to synthesize information from the text
    D. help students to visualize the concepts and terms in the text

The correct answer is A. Establishing a purpose for reading, the foundation for a reading unit or activity, is intimately connected to activating the students' prior knowledge in strategic ways. When the reason for reading is developed in the context of the students' experiences, they are far better prepared to succeed because they can make connections from a base they thoroughly understand. This influences motivation, and with proper motivation, students are more enthused and put forward more effort to understand the text. The other choices are only indirectly supported by this activity and are more specific in focus.

TEACHER CERTIFICATION STUDY GUIDE

25. **Among junior-high school students of low-to-average readability levels, which work would most likely stir reading interest? (Skill 1.6) (Rigorous)**

    A. *Elmer Gantry*, Sinclair Lewis
    B. *Smiley's People*, John Le Carre
    C. *The Outsiders*, S.E. Hinton
    D. *And Then There Were None*, Agatha Christie.

The answer is C. The students can easily identify with the characters, the social issues, the vocabulary, and the themes in the book. The book deals with teenage concerns such as fitting-in, cliques, and appearance in ways that have proven very engaging for young readers.

26. **Students are fluent readers if they (Skill 1.6) (Rigorous)**

    A. read texts fast enough and with appropriate expression, or prosody.
    B. read word-to-word and haltingly.
    C. must intentionally decode a majority of the words.
    D. write disorganized sentences

The correct answer is A. A fluent reader reads words accurately, at target speeds, and with appropriate expression. It is a positive term. The other choices describe negative outcomes.

27. **Reading assessment should take place (Skill 1.6) (Rigorous)**

    A. At the end of the semester.
    B. At the end of a unit.
    C. Constantly.
    D. All of the above.

The correct answer is D. End-of-unit and end-of-semester measurements yield important information regarding achievement of course objectives and the evaluating of students' growth; however, assessment should be going on all the time so that the teacher can adjust instruction to meet the day-to-day needs of the students.

TEACHER CERTIFICATION STUDY GUIDE

28. Which of the following approaches is *not* useful in assessing slower or immature readers? (Skill 1.6) (Rigorous)

    A. Repeated readings.
    B. Echo reading.
    C. Wide reading.
    D. Reading content that is more difficult than their skill levels in order to "stretch" their abilities.

The correct answer is D. Reading content for such students should be at a level where they can read and understand the word nuances, not at a level beyond such understanding and competence. Repeated readings of appropriate material builds this foundation. So does echo reading, or listening to a skilled reader and then trying to imitate his or her delivery. Wide reading is an approach intended to motivate students to read for pleasure and information from a variety of sources and involving socially-motivating processing routines.

29. A teacher should refer all of the following concerns to the appropriate expert <u>except for</u> (Skill 1.6) (Rigorous)

    A. Auditory trauma.
    B. Ear infection.
    C. Vision problems.
    D. Underdeveloped vocabulary.

The answer is D. The teacher is the expert in vocabulary development. The other choices require a medical professional.

30. Middle-School students bring little, if any, initial experience in (Skill 1.6) (Rigorous)

    A. Phonics.
    B. Phonemics.
    C. Textbook reading assignments.
    D. Stories read by the teacher.

The correct answer is C. In middle school, probably for the first time, the student will be expected to read textbook assignments and come to class prepared to discuss the content. Students get phonics (the systematic study of decoding) in the early grades, and they normally get phonemics (familiarity with the syllable sounds of English) even earlier. They will have almost certainly had stories read to them by a teacher by the time they get to middle school.

31. **To enhance reading comprehension, experts recommend all of these techniques except for (Skill 1.6) (Rigorous)**

    A. Read material through only once, but read slowly and carefully.
    B. Read material through more than once according to a plan.
    C. Create a map for the next reading.
    D. Highlight or take notes during reading.

The correct answer is A. While reading at a rate that assures accuracy is desirable, there is no evidence to support a recommendation to avoid rereading something. Choice B is advisable because it proposes a purpose for the rereadings. Choice C is advisable because it also addresses purpose. Choice D is advisable because it helps students maintain focus as they read.

32. **The most significant drawback to applying learning theory research to classroom practice is that (Skill 1.6) (Rigorous)**

    A. today's students do not acquire reading skills with the same alacrity as when greater emphasis was placed on reading classical literature.
    B. development rates are complicated by geographical and cultural differences that are difficult to overcome.
    C. homogeneous grouping has contributed to faster development of some age groups.
    D. social and environmental conditions have contributed to an escalated maturity level than research done twenty or more years ago would seem to indicate.

The answer is D. A mismatch exists between what interests today's students and the learning materials presented to them. Choice A is a significant problem only if the school insists on using classical literature exclusively. Choice B does describe a drawback, but students are more alike in their disengagement from anachronistic learning materials than they are different due to their culture and geographical location. Choice C describes a situation that is not widespread.

33. The students in Mrs. Cline's seventh grade language arts class were invited to attend a performance of *Romeo and Juliet* presented by the drama class at the high school. To best prepare, they should (Skill 1.6) (Rigorous)

    A. read the play as a homework exercise.
    B. read a synopsis of the plot and a biographical sketch of the author.
    C. examine a few main selections from the play to become familiar with the language and style of the author.
    D. read a condensed version of the story and practice attentive listening skills.

The answer is D. By reading a condensed version of the play, students will know the plot and therefore be better able to follow the play on stage. They will also practice being attentive. Choice A is far less dynamic and few will do it. Choice B is likewise dull. Choice C is not thorough enough.

34. Which aspect of language is innate? (Skill 1.6) (Average)

    A. Biological capability to articulate sounds understood by other humans
    B. Cognitive ability to create syntactical structures
    C. Capacity for using semantics to convey meaning in a social environment
    D. Ability to vary inflections and accents

The answer is A. The biological capability to articulate sounds understood by other humans is innate; and, later, children learn semantics and syntactical structures through trial and error. Linguists agree that language is first a vocal system of word symbols that enable a human to communicate his or her feelings, thoughts, and desires to other human beings.

35. Which of the following reading strategies calls for higher order cognitive skills? (Skill 1.6) (Rigorous)

    A. making predictions
    B. summarizing
    C. skimming
    D. making inferences

The answer is D. Making inferences from a reading text involves using other reading skills such as making predictions, skimming, scanning, summarizing, then coming to conclusions or making inferences which are not directly stated in the text.

TEACHER CERTIFICATION STUDY GUIDE

36. The most effective strategy for learning vocabulary is (Skill 1.6) (Rigorous)

   A. memorizing lists
   B. guessing from context
   C. finding words in the dictionary
   D. researching the word's history

The correct answer is B. Guessing vocabulary from context is the most effective method for learning vocabulary as the learner is able to make associations with other familiar words and construct units of meaning, rather than learning isolated word that may be easily forgotten.

37. Which of the following bits of information best describes the structure of English? (Skill 2.1) (Average)

   A. Syntax based on word order.
   B. Inflected.
   C. Romantic.
   D. Orthography is phonetic.

The correct answer is A. The syntax of English, reflective of its Germanic origins, relies on word order rather than inflection. Because of this and the many influences of other languages (particularly with regard to vocabulary), the orthography is not phonetic, which complicates the teaching of standardized spelling.

38. Which of the following sentences contains an error in agreement? (Skill 2.1) (Easy)

   A. Jennifer is one of the women who writes for the magazine.
   B. Each one of their sons plays a different sport.
   C. This band has performed at the Odeum many times.
   D. The data are available online at the listed website.

The correct answer is A. "Women" is the plural antecedent of the relative pronoun "who," which is functioning as the subject in its clause; so "who" is plural and requires the 3rd person plural form for the verb: "write."

39. Which group of words is not a sentence? (Skill 2.1) (Easy)

    A. In keeping with the graduation tradition, the students, in spite of the rain, standing in the cafeteria tossing their mortarboards.
    B. Rosa Parks, who refused to give up her seat on the bus, will be forever remembered for her courage.
    C. Taking advantage of the goalie's being out of the net, we scored our last and winning goal.
    D. When it began to rain, we gathered our possessions and ran for the pavilion.

The correct answer is A. This is a sentence fragment because sentences require a subject and a verb and there is no verb. Changing "the students, in spite of the rain, standing" to "the students, in spite of the rain, were standing" corrects the problem.

40. Identify the sentence that has an error in parallel structure. (Skill 2.1) (Easy)

    A. In order to help your favorite cause, you should contribute time or money, raise awareness, and write congressmen.
    B. Many people envision scientists working alone in a laboratory and discovering scientific breakthroughs.
    C. Some students prefer watching videos to textbooks because they are used to visual presentation.
    D. Tom Hanks, who has won two Academy Awards, is celebrated as an actor, director, and producer.

The answer is C. Parallel structure means that certain sentence structures in key positions match-up grammatically. In choice C, "watching videos" is a gerund phrase functioning as the direct object of the verb, and, because the verb implies a comparison, parallel construction requires that "textbooks" (functioning as the object of a currently-missing gerund) be preceded by an appropriate gerund--in this case, "reading." In order for the structure to be parallel, the sentence should read "Some students prefer watching videos to reading textbooks because they are used to visual presentation." They prefer something to something else. The other sentences conform to parallel structure. Recognizing parallel structure requires a sophisticated understanding of grammar.

41. **Which of the following sentences is unambiguously properly punctuated? (Skill 2.1) (Average)**

    A. The more you eat; the more you want.
    B. The authors—John Steinbeck, Ernest Hemingway, and William Faulkner—are staples of modern writing in American literature textbooks.
    C. Handling a wild horse, takes a great deal of skill and patience
    D. The man, who replaced our teacher, is a comedian.

The answer is B. Dashes should be used instead of commas when commas are used elsewhere in the sentence for amplification or explanation—here within the dashes. Choice A has a semicolon where there should be a comma. Choice C has a comma that shouldn't be there at all. Choice D could be correct in a non-restrictive context, and so whether or not it is correct is ambiguous.

42. **A punctuation mark indicating omission, interrupted thought, or an incomplete statement is a/an (Skill 2.1) (Average)**
    A. ellipsis.
    B. anachronism.
    C. colloquy.
    D. idiom

The answer is A. In an ellipsis, a word or words that would clarify the sentence's message are missing, yet it is still possible to understand them from the context. An anachronism is something out of its proper time frame. A colloquy is a formal conversation or dialogue. An idiom is a saying peculiar to some language group.

43. **Which of the following contains an error in possessive punctuation? (Skill 2.1) (Easy)**

    A. Doris's shawl
    B. mother's-in-law frown
    C. children's lunches
    D. ambassador's briefcase

The answer is B. Mother-in-law is a compound common noun, and the apostrophe should come at the end of the word, according to convention. The other choices are correctly punctuated.

44. Which level of meaning is the hardest aspect of a language to master? (Skill 2.2) (Rigorous)

   A. denotation
   B. jargon
   C. connotation
   D. slang

The answer is C. Connotation refers to the meanings suggested by a word, rather than the dictionary definition. For example, the word 'slim' means thin, and it is usually used with a positive connotation, to compliment of admire someone's figure. The word 'skinny' also means thin, but its connotations are not as flattering as those of the word 'slim'. The connotative aspect of language is more difficult to master than the denotation (dictionary definition), as the former requires a mastery of the social aspect of language, not just the linguistic rules.

45. This statement, "I'll die if I don't pass this course," exemplifies a/an (Skill 2.2) (Easy)

   A. barbarism.
   B. oxymoron.
   C. hyperbole.
   D. antithesis.

The answer is C. A hyperbole is an exaggeration for the sake of emphasis. It is a figure of speech not meant to be taken literally. A barbarism is the use of incorrect or unacceptable language. An oxymoron is a term comprised of opposite or incongruous elements, such as peace fighter.

46. Read the following passage:

   "It would have been hard to find a passer-by more wretched in appearance. He was a man of middle height, stout and hardy, in the strength of maturity; he might have been forty-six or seven. A slouched leather cap hid half his face, bronzed by the sun and wind, and dripping with sweat."

   What is its main form of discourse? (Skill 2.2) (Easy)

   A. Description
   B. Narration
   C. Exposition
   D. Persuasion

The answer is A. The passage describes the appearance of a person in detail. Narration tells a story. Exposition explains or informs. Persuasion promotes a point of view or course of action.

47. Consider the following sentence:

Mr. Brown is a school volunteer <u>with a reputation and twenty years service</u>.

Which phrase below best represents the logical intent of the underlined phrase above? (Choice E is identical to the underlined phrase) (Skill 2.2) (Rigorous)

A. with a reputation for twenty years' service
B. with a reputation for twenty year's service
C. who has served twenty years
D. with a service reputation of twenty years

The correct answer is D. His reputation pertains to his service performance, not its duration. Choice A implies that it was for its duration. Choice B has Choice A's problem plus an incorrectly punctuated possessive. Choice C ignores his service reputation. Choice E is extremely vague.

48. Consider the following sentence:

Joe <u>didn't hardly know his cousin Fred</u>, who'd had a rhinoplasty.

Which word group below best conveys the intended meaning of the underlined section above? (Skill 2.2) (Average)

A. hardly did know his cousin Fred
B. didn't know his cousin Fred hardly
C. hardly knew his cousin Fred
D. didn't know his cousin Fred

The correct answer is C. It contains a correctly-phrased negative expressed in the appropriate tense. Choice A has tense and awkwardness problems. Choice B has tense and double-negative problems. Choice D ignores the fact that he knew Fred a little. Choice E has tense and double-negative problems

49. The substitution of "went to his rest" for "died" exemplifies a/an (Skill 2.2) (Easy)

    A. bowdlerism.
    B. jargon.
    C. euphemism.
    D. malapropism.

The answer is C. A euphemism alludes to a distasteful topic in a pleasant manner in order to obscure or soften the disturbing impact of the original. A bowdlerism is a prudish version of something. Jargon is language specific to some occupation or activity. A Malapropism is the improper use of a word that sounds like the word that would fit the context. The result is most often ludicrous.

50. The arrangement and relationship of words in sentences or sentence structures best describes (Skill 2.2) (Average)

    A. style.
    B. discourse.
    C. thesis.
    D. syntax.

The answer is D. Syntax is the grammatical structure of sentences. Style is not limited to considerations of syntax only, but includes vocabulary, voice, genre, and other language features. Discourse refers to investigating some idea. A thesis is a statement of opinion.

51. Which aspect of language shows the most evident change over time? (Skill 2.3) (Average)

    A. phonetics
    B. vocabulary
    C. syntax
    D. spelling

The answer is B. History has shown that languages are more open to accepting new words than they are to making rule changes to phonetics, grammar or spelling.

TEACHER CERTIFICATION STUDY GUIDE

52. The Old English period refers to (Skill 2.3) (Average)

    A. The Fourth Century
    B. The Third through the Eighth Century
    C. The Fifth through the Tenth Century
    D. The Fifth through the Eighth Century

The correct answer is C. The Old English period begins with the settlement of the British Isles in the fifth and sixth centuries by Germanic tribes and continues until the time of Chaucer.

53. What factor below introduced Modern English? (Skill 2.3) (Rigorous)

    A. The Great Vowel Shift
    B. The printing press
    C. The invasion of the Normans
    D. Phonetic spelling

The correct answer is A. The Great Vowel Shift created guidelines for spelling and pronunciation in the wake of the invention of the printing press. Other answer choices, though related to the question, do not answer it as specifically.

54. Which of the following is not true about English? (Skill 2.3) (Rigorous)

    A. English is the easiest language to learn.
    B. English is the least inflected language.
    C. English has the most extensive vocabulary of any language.
    D. English originated as a Germanic tongue.

The answer is A. English has its own inherent quirks which make it difficult to learn, plus it has incorporated words, ands even structures, from many disparate language groups in its lexicon and syntax. Languages with lexicons limited to words governed by a consistent set of relatively simple rules exist, so English is certainly not the easiest language to learn.

55. If a student uses slang and expletives, what is the best course of action to take in order to improve the student's formal communication skills? (Skill 3.1) (Rigorous)

    A. ask the student to rephrase their writing; that is, translate it into language appropriate for the school principal to read.
    B. refuse to read the student's papers until he conforms to a more literate style.
    C. ask the student to read his work aloud to the class for peer evaluation.
    D. rewrite the flagrant passages to show the student the right form of expression.

The answer is A. Asking the student to write to the principal, a respected authority figure, will alert the student to the need to use formal language. Simply refusing to read the paper is not only negative, it also sets up a power struggle. Asking the student to read slang and expletives aloud to the class for peer evaluation is to risk unproductive classroom chaos and to support the class clowns. Rewriting the flagrant passages for the student to model formal expression does not immerse the student in the writing process.

56. Oral debate is most closely associated with which form of discourse? (Skill 3.1) (Average)

    A. Description
    B. Exposition
    C. Narration
    D. Persuasion

The answer is D. The purpose of a debate is to convince some audience or set of judges about something, which is very much the same as persuading some audience or set of judges about something.

57. A composition with no voice will lack the following quality (Skill 3.1) (Rigorous)

    A. organization
    B. appeal
    C. illustrations
    D. ideas

The answer is B. Voice in writing refers to an author's tone, point of view or manner of communicating. A composition may have good ideas, organization and illustrations or example, but without voice, it will lack character and will not be appealing reading.

58. **A conversation between two or more people is called a/an (Skill 3.1) (Easy)**

    A. parody.
    B. dialogue.
    C. monologue.
    D. analogy.

The answer is B. Dialogues are the conversations virtually indispensable to dramatic work, and they often appear in narrative and poetry, as well. A parody is a work that adopts the subject and structure of another work in order to ridicule it. A monologue is a work or part of a work written in the first person. An analogy illustrates an idea by means of a more familiar one that is similar or parallel to it.

59. **To explain or to inform belongs in the category of (Skill 3.1) (Average)**

    A. exposition.
    B. narration.
    C. persuasion.
    D. description.

The answer is A. Exposition sets forth a systematic explanation of any subject and informs the audience about various topics. It can also introduce the characters of a story and their situations as the story begins. Narration tells a story. Persuasion seeks to influence an audience so that they will adopt some new point of view or take some action. Description provides sensory details and addresses spatial relationships of objects.

60. **Varying the complexity of a graphic organizer exemplifies differentiating which aspect of a lesson? (Skill 3.1) (Rigorous)**

    A. its content/topic
    B. its environment
    C. its process
    D. its product

The correct answer is C. Differentiating the process means offering a variety of learning activities or strategies to students as they manipulate the ideas embedded within the lesson concept. For example, students may use graphic organizers, maps, diagrams, or charts to display their comprehension of concepts covered. Varying the complexity of a graphic organizer can very effectively accommodate differing levels of cognitive processing so that students of differing ability are appropriately engaged. Lesson topic and content remain the same, the lesson is still taking place in the same environment, and, in most lessons, the graphic organizer is not the product of the lesson.

61. Modeling is a practice that requires students to (Skill 3.1) (Average)

   A. create a style unique to their own language capabilities.
   B. emulate the writing of professionals.
   C. paraphrase passages from good literature.
   D. peer evaluate the writings of other students.

The answer is B. Modeling engages students in analyzing the writing of professional writers and in imitating the syntactical, grammatical and stylistic mastery of that writer. Choice A is an issue of voice. Choice C is a less rigorous form of the correct answer. Choice D is only very indirectly related to modeling.

62. In a timed essay test of an hour's duration, how much time should be devoted to prewriting. (Skill 3.1) (Easy)

   A. five
   B. ten
   C. fifteen
   D. twenty

The answer is B. Ten minutes of careful planning still allows sufficient time for the other stages of the writing process. Five minutes would result more dead-ends and backtracking. Fifteen and twenty minutes would result in rushing drafting, revising, and editing.

63. A student informative composition should consist of a minimum of how many paragraphs? (Skill 3.1) (Easy)

   A. three
   B. four
   C. five
   D. six

The answer is C. This composition would consist of an introductory paragraph, three body paragraphs, and a concluding paragraph. A three or four paragraph composition could include all three types of paragraphs, but would not require the students to elaborate at sufficient length in the body of the paper. A six paragraph minimum is slightly excessive, more or less by tradition.

64. **Which of the following is the least effective procedure for promoting consciousness of audience? (Skill 3.1) (Rigorous)**

    A. Pairing students during the writing process
    B. Reading all rough drafts before the students write the final copies
    C. Having students compose stories or articles for publication in school literary magazines or newspapers
    D. Writing letters to friends or relatives

The answer is B. Reading all rough drafts will do the least to promote consciousness of audience; they are very used to turning papers into the teacher, and most don't think much about impressing the teacher. Pairing students will ensure a small, constant audience about whom they care; and having them compose stories for literary magazines will encourage them to put their best efforts forward because their work will be read by an actual audience in an impressive format. Writing letters also engages students in thinking about how best to communicate with a particular audience.

65. **Which of the following is not a technique of prewriting? (Skill 3.1) (Average)**

    A. Clustering
    B. Listing
    C. Brainstorming
    D. Proofreading

The answer is D. You cannot proofread something that you have not yet written. While it is true that prewriting involves written techniques, prewriting is not concerned with punctuation, capitalization, and spelling (proofreading). Brainstorming is a general term denoting generating ideas, and clustering and listing are specific methods of brainstorming.

66. **Writing ideas quickly without interruption of the flow of thoughts or attention to conventions is called (Skill 3.1) (Easy)**

    A. brainstorming.
    B. mapping.
    C. listing.
    D. Free writing.

The answer is D. Free writing is a particular type of brainstorming (techniques to generate ideas). Mapping is another type and results in products resembling flow charts. Listing is another brainstorming technique that differs from free writing in that free writing is more open-ended and looks more like sentences.

67. Computer-assisted instruction (CAI) accommodates all of the following factors in reading instruction *except for* (Skill 3.2) (Average)

   A. free-form responses to comprehension questions
   B. increased motivation
   C. the addition of speech with computer-presented text
   D. the use of computers for word processing, and the integration of writing instruction with reading

The correct answer is A. CAI does not accommodate free-form responses to comprehension questions, and relies heavily on drill-and-practice and multiple-choice formats. This is a limitation of CAI.

68. Which of the four underlined sections of the following sentence contains an error that a word processing spellchecker probably *wouldn't* catch? (Skill 3.2)

   He *tuc* the *hors* by the *rains* and pulled it back to the *stabel*. (Skill 3.2) (Rigorous)

   A. tuc
   B. hors
   C. rains
   D. stable

The answer is C. Rains is a formal word which the spellchecker would have missed even though this sentence is looking for the word reigns.

69. In the hierarchy of needs for adolescents who are becoming more team-oriented in their approach to learning, which need do they exhibit most? (Skill 3.2) (Rigorous)

   A. Need for competence
   B. Need for love/acceptance
   C. Need to know
   D. Need to belong

The answer is B. Abraham's Maslow's theory of Humanistic Development that such older children and adolescents exhibit most a need for love/acceptance from peers and potential romantic partners. Their need for competence is in the service of gaining the love/acceptance. Their need to know is developing, but is not their primary issue. Their need to belong does not address their emerging sexual identities.

70. **Overcrowded classes prevent the individual attention needed to facilitate language development. This drawback can be best overcome by (Skill 3.2) (Rigorous)**

    A. Dividing the class into independent study groups.
    B. Assigning more study time at home.
    C. Using more drill practice in class.
    D. Team teaching.

The answer is A. Dividing a class into small groups maximizes opportunities for engagement. Assigning more study time at home is passing the buck. Using more drill practice in class is likely to bore most students to tears. Team teaching begs the question; if you can get another teacher, then your class should no longer be overcrowded.

71. **All of the following techniques are used to conduct ongoing informal assessment of student progress except for (Skill 3.3) (Average)**

    A. analyzing the student work product at key stages
    B. collecting data from assessment tests
    C. posing strategic questions
    D. observing students as they work

The answer is B. The key here hinges on the adjective, "informal." Assessment tests employ standardized materials and formats to monitor student progress and to report it in statistical terms. The other choices are relatively informal, teacher-specific techniques addressing more current-lesson-specific products and dynamics.

72. **Effective assessment requires that (Skill 3.3) (Rigorous)**

    A. Students not be involved in the assessment process.
    B. Testing activities are kept separate from the teaching activities.
    C. References materials that classroom instruction has prepared the students to read.
    D. Tests, in order to be reliable, should never use materials previously studied in the classroom

The correct answer is C. The only reliable measure of the success of a unit will be based on the reading the instruction has focused on. Choice A makes almost no sense; students will at the very least have to do something that can be assessed. Choice B calls into question the whole reason for schools. Choice D uses different phrases to accomplish the same unworthy end as Choice B.

TEACHER CERTIFICATION STUDY GUIDE

73. **Effective assessment means that (Skill 3.3) (Rigorous)**

    A. It ignores age and cultural considerations
    B. Students' weaknesses are emphasized.
    C. Only reading skills count.
    D. It is integrated with instruction and is not intrusive.

The correct answer is D. Effective assessment informs instruction and practice. It is one phase of an integrated instructional cycle. Choice A ignores reality and distorts rather than informs. Choice B discourages students. Choice C ignores other important ways of demonstrating growth in understanding.

74. **Reading a piece of student writing to assess the overall impression of the product is (Skill 3.3) (Easy)**

    A. holistic evaluation.
    B. portfolio assessment.
    C. analytical evaluation.
    D. using a performance system.

The answer is A. In holistic scoring, the teacher reads quickly through a paper once to get a general impression and assigns a rating based on a rubric that includes the criteria for achievement in a few, key dimensions of the assignment. Portfolio assessment involves tracking work over stages or over time. Analytical evaluation involves breaking down the assignment into discrete traits and determining achievement in each of those traits. A performance system refers to engaging students in writing assignments meant to generate products in a given time frame. Often, such products are scored holistically.

75. **A formative evaluation of student writing (Skill 3.3) (Easy)**

    A. requires a thorough marking of mechanical errors with a pencil or pen.
    B. makes comments on the appropriateness of the student's interpretation of the prompt and the degree to which the objective was met.
    C. requires the student to hand in all the materials produced during the process of writing.
    D. involves several careful readings of the text for content, mechanics, spelling, and usage.

The answer is B. Formative evaluations should support the students' writing process through strategic feedback at key points. Teacher comments and feedback should encourage recursive revision and metacognition. Choice A applies, if anywhere, to a summative evaluation of student writing. Choice C is a neutral management strategy. A teacher can make formative evaluations without collecting all the materials. Choice D, again, is more suited for summative evaluation or for the very last issue in the composition process, namely proofreading.

76. What type of comprehension do questions beginnings with "who," "what," "where," or "how" assess? (Skill 3.4) (Average)

   A. evaluative
   B. inferential
   C. literal
   D. narrative

The correct answer is C. Literal questions ask for facts from the reading. The student can put his finger right on the answer and prove that he is correct. These questions are sometimes referred to as "right there" questions. Evaluative questions require a judgment of some sort. Inferential questions ask students to make an educated guess. Narrative questions involve aspects of a story beyond literal considerations.

77. A paper explaining the relationship between food and weight gain contains the signal words "because," "consequently," "this is how," and "due to." These words suggest that the paper has which text structure? (Skill 3.4) (Average)

   A. cause and effect structure
   B. compare and contrast structure
   C. descriptive structure
   D. sequential structure

The answer is A. These signal words connect events in a causal chain, creating an explanation of some process or event. Compare and contrast structure presents similarities and differences. Descriptive structure presents a sensory impression of something or someone. Sequential structure references what comes first, next, last, and so on.

78. A paper written in first person and having characters, a setting, a plot, some dialogue, and events sequenced chronologically with some flashbacks exemplifies which genre? (Skill 3.4) (Average)

   A. exposition
   B. narration
   C. persuasion
   D. speculation

The answer is B. narration.

79. In 'inverted triangle' introductory paragraphs, the thesis sentence occurs (Skill 3.4) (Easy)

    A. at the beginning of the paragraph.
    B. in the middle of the paragraph.
    C. at the end of the paragraph.
    D. in the second paragraph.

The answer is C. The beginning of the paragraph should establish interest, the middle of the paragraph should establish a general context, and the paragraph should end with the thesis that the rest of the paper will develop. Delaying the thesis until the second paragraph would be 'outside the triangle.'

80. Which of the following should not be included in the opening paragraph of an informative essay? (Skill 3.4) (Average)

    A. Thesis sentence
    B. Details and examples supporting the main idea
    C. broad general introduction to the topic
    D. A style and tone that grabs the reader's attention

The answer is B. The introductory paragraph should introduce the topic, capture the reader's interest, state the thesis and prepare the reader for the main points in the essay. Details and examples, however, belong in the second part of the essay, the body paragraphs.

XAMonline, INC. 21 Orient Ave. Melrose, MA 02176

Toll Free number 800-509-4128

TO ORDER Fax 781-662-9268 OR www.XAMonline.com

PRAXIS SERIES   - PRAXIS - 2009

Address:

City, State Zip

Credit card number_____-_____-_____-_____   expiration_____

EMAIL _____

PHONE   FAX

13# ISBN 2009	TITLE	Qty	Retail	Total
978-1-60787-043-2	Art Sample Test 10133			
978-1-60787-031-9	Biology 20231, 20232, 20235			
978-1-58197-691-5	Chemistry 20241 20242, 20245			
978-1-60787-046-3	Earth and Space Sciences 20571			
978-1-60787-033-3	Special Education: Knowledge-Based Core Principles 20351			
978-1-60787-037-1	Special Education: Teaching Students with Behavioral Disorders/Emotional Disturbance 0371			
978-1-60787-035-7	PRAXIS Early Childhood 020, 022			
978-1-60787-041-8	Educational Leadership 0410			
978-1-60787-048-7	Elementary Education 0011, 0012, 0014, 0016			
978-1-60787-044-9	English Language, Literature, and Composition 10041			
978-1-60787-053-1	French Sample Test 0173			
978-1-60787-042-5	Fundamental Subjects 0511			
978-1-60787-032-6	School Guidance & Counseling 20420			
978-1-58197-268-9	General Science 10435			
978-1-60787-039-5	Library Media Specialist 0310			
978-1-60787-049-4	Mathematics 10061, 20063			
978-1-58197-269-6	Middle School English Language Arts 10049			
978-1-58197-343-3	Middle School Mathematics 20069			
978-1-58197-263-4	Middle School Social Studies 0089			
978-1-60787-040-1	Physical Education 10091			
978-1-60787-047-0	Physics 0265			
978-1-60787-038-8	ParaPro Assessment 0755			
978-1-60787-036-4	PPST I: Basic Skills 0710, 0720, 0730			
978-1-58197-054-8	Government/Poltical Science 10930			
978-1-58197-577-2	Principals of Learning and Teaching 30521, 30522, 30523,			
978-1-60787-034-0	Reading 0200, 0201, 0202			
978-1-58197-696-0	Social Studies 10081			
978-1-58197-718-9	Spanish 10191, 30194			
978-1-60787-057-9	353 Exceptional Student Core Content Knowledge (New)			
978-1-60787-055-5	382 Education of Exceptional Students - Learning Disability			
978-1-60787-056-2	542 Ed Students Disabilities Mild to Moderate disabilities			
	Shipping $8.70 1 book, $11.00 2 books, $15.00 3			
	TOTAL			